BRAVE

ADELE BELLIS

HarperElement
An imprint of HarperCollins*Publishers*
1 London Bridge Street
London SE1 9GF

www.harpercollins.co.uk

First published by HarperElement 2016

3 5 7 9 10 8 6 4

A catalogue record of this book is
available from the British Library

ISBN 978-0-00-818209-0

Printed and bound in Great Britain by
Clays Ltd, St Ives plc

MIX
Paper from
responsible sources

FSC
www.fsc.org
FSC™ C007454

CONTENTS

CONTENTS

PROLOGUE

There was smoke, I remember that. As I ran into the road, my body consumed by pain, my flesh, my hair, my clothes were actually smoking. The rest of it still comes to me in flashes ... The eyes of my assailant, a look of pure evil in those deep, dark pupils buried between his hoody and the black scarf covering his mouth and nose.

I can still remember those first horrifying split seconds, that exact moment when I realised that the liquid that was dripping down my hair and through my skin wasn't water, but something much, much worse. And by the time my brain had scrambled enough sense to find a name for it – acid – every nerve in my body was screaming in pain.

I remember the old woman who I ran to. Moments before, she had just been any other person waiting for a bus and she could now have been my saviour. Except that when I grabbed her hands, pleading – begging – for her to help me, she looked down at her own flesh where the acid from my skin had seeped into hers and she cried out terrified as she watched her own flesh disappear.

I remember screaming for water.

I remember running into the road, weaving among the traffic, trying to get away from myself.

I remember feeling my ear melting from my face. I remember the sense of it shrinking and shrivelling on the side of my head. And the smell, I remember the smell, but I couldn't describe it here on these pages. The smell of your own face melting is not something anyone should ever have to attempt to conjure up in their mind. Not that part of an act of pure evil.

Yet among all that pain, that searing, scorching-level pain, I knew exactly who was responsible. My brain cut through that raging heat, the white fire that seemed to engulf every nerve in my body and reminded me of one name.

I remember that name more than anything.

I was struggling so hard to survive, just to live, not to melt away, although that's what I was doing in that moment; running like a wild woman into the road, seeing the horrified faces of strangers who had stopped to help and now ran from me to save their own skin. Literally.

But say I'd been able to pause that scene. Say I could have stopped it there and then, just for a minute, just for a second, I could have had one logical thought that wasn't consumed by pain. I've no doubt as to what it would have been. I would have thought: how did our love come to this?

CHAPTER 1

INTENSITY

'Mum, can I borrow a tenner?'

She glanced at me quickly and then back at *Coronation Street*.

'Pass me my bag, Adele,' she said.

I hovered beside her as she fished around in her handbag for her purse, the scent of my Calvin Klein perfume filling our small living room. But just as she pulled her black leather purse from her bag, just as she was about to flip it open, she looked up at me.

'Where are you going?'

'Bowling.'

I tried to sound casual, looking straight ahead at the TV, but I still saw her give me a quick scan up and down: thick mascara, pink glossy lips, long dark hair falling down my back, stringy top, jeans …

'In heels?' she asked.

I shot a quick glance at my dad then, but luckily his eyes were fixed on the TV. When I turned back to Mum, I saw that her eyebrows were raised, awaiting an answer, the hint of a smile curling at the corner of her lips.

'Yeah, I'll hire bowling shoes when I get there.'

She looked at me for a second before shaking her head, turning back to her purse and pulling out a crisp £10 note.

'There. Have fun,' she said, putting it in my hand. '… And be careful!' she called after me.

As I picked up my overnight bag by the front door, I couldn't resist a smile because, of course, I had no intention at all of going to the bowling alley; that was the kind of thing I did when I was 14. Now I was 16, and me and my friends had already figured out which pubs we could get served at.

Seconds later I'd left our red-brick terraced home, the blueish light from the television flickering behind our bay window as I hurried down the front path towards the bus stop.

I felt my phone buzz in my pocket.

Just got on the bus.
C u soon x

My friend Laura Woodcock. I was staying at hers tonight and we lived on the same bus route into town. She always texted me when she got on the bus so we could travel into town together.

The bus stop was a short walk from our house – a route I'd taken so many times in my life because this house was the only home I'd ever known. I'd first toddled this route when I was tiny, my hand in Mum's, my older brothers Adam and Scott trailing alongside us, but these days I'd hurry along to it in my heels and whatever outfit I'd planned for my night out.

I felt the fresh crunch of the £10 note inside my palm and smiled to myself again. As the youngest, and the only girl in a family of two boys, I was used to getting my own way. For as far back as I could remember I'd always been a daddy's girl. My dad worked long hours as a self-employed painter and decorator, but he always had time for me. He'd spoil me rotten too: whenever we went shopping and I snuck some chocolate into the trolley, Mum would always tell me to put it back on the shelf, but I only had to whinge to Dad and it would be mine.

'Kevin!' Mum would moan at him.

'Oh come on, Colleen, it's just a bar of chocolate.'

And I'd grin to myself.

My brothers have tormented me my entire life, as older brothers do, from practising their WWE moves on me when I was eight or nine, in my knee-high white socks and hair-bands, to throwing my dolly out of the pram onto the floor just to tease me. But all I had to do was shout 'Mum!' and they'd get told off.

'Leave your sister alone!' Mum would shout through from the kitchen.

I'd quickly realised that being the little sister made me almost invincible. But it wasn't always me that got the better of them. With all male cousins too, I'd often get left out of their games growing up. I'd run behind them, hoping they'd let me climb trees alongside them on sunny days when we'd have a picnic down at Toby Walk, but often they'd run too fast for my little legs to keep up. It had made me try harder, develop a tougher skin, be feisty when I needed to be. But that wasn't a bad thing.

The bus rounded the corner as I noticed that the sky had deepened to a deep blue since I'd left the house, and illuminated by the lights inside the bus I saw Laura waving to me. I got on and took a seat next to her.

'All right?'

She'd put her jeans and a strappy top on too but I wasn't sure why either of us had dressed up. We didn't really fancy a big night tonight.

'I'm knackered,' Laura yawned.

'Me too,' I said, catching her tiredness. 'I can't be bothered to drink tonight.'

'Me neither,' she said. 'Let's just pop to the pub for a couple of hours, though. It's something to do.'

The last few weeks had been full of new starts for me. School had finished in the summer, and I'd got my GCSE results. They were OK, enough to get me on the beauty course at Lowestoft College. I hadn't been a swot at school, I'd done enough to get by, but for me it was all about my social life. I'd made some great friends there – Jade, Remi, Paige, Becca, Madison and Jessie – while Laura was an old friend from middle school.

We were a pretty tight-knit group: we'd grown up together, hanging around in the local park each night after school, pooling our money and convincing strangers to buy us a bottle of vodka from the corner shop or a packet of Mayfair Superkings. We'd hang out there until 10 or 11 when we all had to be home, but on a Friday night – once my parents had gone out – I'd usually sneak back out to a friend's house. There we'd spend the rest of the evening texting boys, or giggling about who'd been snogging who in the park while the boys practised their wheelies around us.

It was all so innocent then, but now life had changed, we were all growing up. Over the summer I'd lost my virginity to a boy. It wasn't anything serious, just kids messing about. I'd met a couple of other girls too, Rachel and Amie, along with another girl, Lauren – who was doing the same beauty course at college as me. I had wanted to be a nurse at one point, but somehow the beauty course had seemed like an easier option. I loved it too, especially the anatomy and physiology, learning all about the skin, the muscles and bones, blood vessels and capillaries.

I was only a few weeks into the course so we were still covering the basics like how to cleanse, tone and moisturise – it wasn't like I wasn't used to doing that each night anyway, the same for painting nails, but it was interesting to learn about cuticles and how to treat them. I really felt different since leaving school, older, more grown up, so it seemed funny that just like any other 16-year-old girl I still borrowed money off my mum and fibbed to her about where I was going. Anyway, it was amazing what I could get out of a tenner – drinks in the pub, a takeaway, a packet of cigarettes and a taxi home. I was never quite sure how I managed it.

This would be a low-key night, though. Me and Laura weren't looking for a big one. We got to the pub, went in and found Amie and our other friends. We actually ended up having a laugh: there was always some gossip to giggle over. I sank one vodka and coke after another, the ice clinking against my teeth as I finished each one, and I always left the bar with that little buzz just because I'd been served. I loved hearing who was snogging who, or who'd broken up that week. It was still like being at school, only better because we could buy our own booze now.

It got to about 11.30 and the atmosphere in the pub changed as people started to talk about moving on and collected their coats and bags to step out into the dark September night.

'Shall we just go home?' I asked Laura, swaying a little as I did. I hadn't noticed just how the drink had gone to my head.

She nodded. But when I opened my purse to see how much I'd got for the taxi home, it was empty and there was nothing in Laura's purse either.

'How did that happen?' I said.

We stared at each other.

I sighed and said, 'We'll just have to go around and ask anyone if they've got a pound to spare for a taxi. We could easily collect a fiver that way.'

So we split up, Laura going one way, me the other. I saw her out of the corner of my eye over on the other side of the pub, strangers shaking their heads and looking at us bemused as we went from one of them to another. Not that we cared, we were high on vodka and cokes, we didn't mind if they thought we were two silly girls who'd spent our cab fare home.

Eventually, though, after so many refusals to help, I got bored. I wandered out the front doors of the pub and into the street where the chill in the air made my head spin with alcohol and reminded me I should have brought a jacket. I decided to warm myself up with a cigarette and fished into my handbag for one, and that was the exact moment that I first laid eyes on Anthony Riley. Not that I noticed him then; I wouldn't have picked him out of a crowd, and of course I didn't know his name either. There was a group of lads standing just a few feet away from me. I recognised them as mates of my brother Scott.

'That's Scott's sister,' I heard one or two of them say, and that's when he looked up.

'All right?' he said, lighting his own cigarette beside me. 'How you doing?'

I noticed him at that moment because his accent was like nothing from round where I lived: there was no Suffolk lilt, he didn't drop his consonants in the same way as we did, didn't stretch his vowels. He spoke with a Scottish accent, and, if nothing else, it piqued my interest.

'I like your accent,' I said, as I took another drag on my fag and with it lungs full of confidence.

He laughed. 'Thanks,' he said, nodding to me with a smile. 'I'm Riley.'

'I'm Adele,' I said. 'You're not from round here.'

'Well done,' he grinned, as I giggled into my cigarette. 'I'm from Glasgow, moved here when I was 15.'

I could see he was older than me by a few years. I'd put him at 19 because of the other lads he was with, the ones who were the same age as my brother.

'Where you off to tonight?' he asked. 'Are you coming with us?'

'Nah, we're just going home now, but we've spent all our taxi money on vodka.'

He laughed again, his green eyes twinkling as he did. His hair was short at the sides, longer on top, spiky, like most of the guys wore it, and he had one tiny hoop earring in his left ear. He was dressed nicely, a blue and red checked shirt, jeans, shoes instead of trainers which meant he was going on to the club. He reminded me of someone famous too, someone from *EastEnders*, but I couldn't think who at the time.

He took another drag on his cigarette and I watched the blue smoke curl up into the air around us, and as he did he reached into his back pocket and pulled out his wallet. He opened it and pulled out a fiver, then handed it to me.

'Here you go,' he said. 'That should get you home.'

'Oh God, really?' I said. 'Are you sure?'

'Aye,' he said. 'Can't have you walking home, can we?'

'Oh thanks so much!'

Laura appeared at my side then, just in time to see me fold the note up and put it into my pocket.

'I can pay you back if you –'

He tutted and shook his head.

'Don't be silly,' he said. 'But you can take my number.'

I smiled then and felt something other than the cigarette go to my head and my heart quicken a little inside my chest.

'OK,' I said, pulling my phone out of my bag.

His mates looked over at us as I started punching his number in.

'Come on, Trevor, we're leaving now,' one called.

He looked up briefly. 'Hang on a sec,' he called to them.

'Trevor?'

'Aye, that's what they call me,' he said with a smile as if I should know why. 'From *EastEnders*? Trevor Morgan. Little Mo's fella?'

'Oh, the crazy Scottish guy!' I said.

'Yeah, original eh?'

'Actually, you do look a bit like him.'

He laughed. 'So are you going to take my number?'

'Oh yeah,' I said, quickly, glancing at his friends over his shoulder waiting to leave with him.

He finished giving me it and I saved it under Riley.

'Thanks again for the fiver,' I said.

'Ach, no problem,' he replied. 'See you again.'

And then he was gone.

Wait, did he say 'again'? Or was it 'around'? And if he said 'again', was it like *again*? Or just something you say. I turned back to Laura. She stood there, eyes wide.

'He was all right, wasn't he?'

'Yeah!' I laughed, and then I remembered the £5 note in my back pocket that this Scottish knight in shining armour had given us. I whipped it out. 'Ta dah!'

'Come on, let's get a taxi,' Laura said.

We followed the lads down the road. They were on the other side, and I couldn't resist watching Riley. They were larking about, bantering with each other, laughing, giving each other the odd playful push off the path, and there was a part of me that wished we were going into the club too. But soon enough we reached the taxi rank, and Laura had given the driver her address. She got in the car, and left the door open for me.

'Well, come on then!' she said.

And I tore my eyes away from that Scottish stranger, just in time to see him disappear into the nightclub. Did he say 'again', or had he said 'around'? I already knew which one I preferred.

If only I had known …

* * *

When we got back to Laura's parents, we went through the whole thing again.

'So I was just standing there having a fag and then he came over ...'

'And then what happened?' Laura said.

I told her everything, all the little details, how he looked, how he said it, how he smiled as he did.

'Do you think it's too soon to text him?' I said. 'I mean, I could just say thanks for the fiver.'

Laura checked the time on her phone. 'It's 12.30,' she said.

'You don't think I'd look desperate?'

'No, I think it's OK.'

So I tried various different messages, some with questions, but that did seem too desperate, others with kisses – too forward – before finally settling on this:

Hope you had a good night,
thanks for the fiver. Adele

Friendly, not too keen. And now I just had to wait. Laura and I sat up for a bit longer, both of us taking it in turns to stare at my phone. I picked it up, turned it over, waiting for it to bleep a reply into my hands, but nothing. Eventually we went to bed.

There wasn't a reply the next day either, or the next.

'Do you think he gave me the right number?' I said to Amie and Lauren during lunch break at college on Monday.

'Why wouldn't he?'

'So why hasn't he replied?'

I felt like I wasn't that bothered on Friday night, I kind of liked him, but I wasn't *that* keen. But a weekend spent staring at my phone had left me with more questions than answers. I'd tried switching it off and on again, but texts from my other friends were still coming through.

'Do you think I should text him again?' I asked the girls.

'No!' they replied in unison.

And so I waited. And waited. And waited.

And just as I'd managed to distract myself on Tuesday, and while we learnt that there are 27 bones in the human hand, my phone beeped in class. Amie shot a look over in my direction and when I saw the name Riley I nodded back to her and felt heat rush to my cheeks.

> Sorry, been on a bender all
> weekend. How are you?

And there it started, right there in my college classroom. I didn't leave it days or even hours to reply to him, not now I had his attention. I wanted to keep up the momentum.

I texted him back, I can't remember what exactly now, I must have made a joke about him being on a bender because he replied straight away, and then I replied back, and it went back and forth like that for days.

I sent the girls a group message on MSN Messenger.

> We're texting all the time!

I felt different even then, perhaps because I knew he was friends with my brother, perhaps it gave it that added element of excitement, that bit of rebellion, and mostly because this guy was new. He wasn't like the other scruffy 16-year-old boys that we hung around with, who were only just getting to grips with shaving. Anthony was 19, he was a man, he didn't hang around parks convincing people to buy him a bottle of booze, he was old enough to buy it himself. He didn't live at home with his mum, he lived with his friend, Scott Tarrant, 'Scotty'. OK, he lived with Scotty's mum, but it wasn't the same as being stuck at home with your parents. He had a job too – or at least he'd had one before: he told me during one of our text messages that he'd been made redundant from his scaffolding job. *And* he could drive, well, he couldn't at the moment because he'd got a ban for speeding, but he was different, he was interesting, even a speeding ban only made him more exciting and dangerous.

And with that accent Anthony felt exotic compared to the lads around here, not just because of his age, but because it felt to me like he'd just appeared out of nowhere. In a town where I pretty much knew most people my age, or certainly knew of them, Anthony had never been anywhere on my radar before – or that of any of my friends – and I liked him for that reason if nothing else. I didn't know where he'd appeared from, I just knew that I liked him, and over the days as we texted and bantered and he made me laugh, I liked him more. And then finally …

> Fancy coming round
> tomorrow night?
>
> > OK.

I told the girls that he'd asked me round to Scotty's place, and as Remi knew Scotty she decided to come too. Not in a double-date way, because this was going to be my date and Remi didn't fancy Scotty, but just so I could get to know Anthony.

The next night I told Mum I was off out with Remi, and then I heard a beep outside the house.

'Take care, Adele,' Mum called after me as I slammed the front door shut behind me.

Scotty had arrived in his green Punto to pick me up, and there in the passenger seat beside him was Anthony.

'All right?' the boys said when I got in the back.

We went from mine to pick up Remi, and then when we got to Scotty's house Jade texted saying she wanted to come over too.

'We'll go and get Jade,' Scotty said, gesturing towards Remi. Did I see a look pass between him and Anthony?

The next moment Anthony and I were alone in the house and all at once the space in the living room between us felt like a mile.

'So ... er ...'

'Yeah,' Anthony replied.

We'd been texting for days and yet suddenly neither of us knew what to say. We were glued inside an awkward silence, made worse by the fact that I realised in those moments just how much I fancied him, and seeing this soft side – this shy side – made him seem even more attractive.

And I think, after a while like that, we both just looked up and fell about laughing at the ridiculousness of it all. And that just made me like him more.

Anthony got me a vodka and coke and I gulped it down to take the edge off my nerves, and so by the time Scotty came back with Remi and Jade we were laughing and messing about. We put some music on, I remember Kings of Leon's 'Sex On Fire' and feeling slightly drunk and very excited just to be in the same room with this older guy with his Scottish accent and his charm and those eyes.

'Shall we watch a film?' one of the boys suggested after a while, and they put something on – not that any of us really watched it as we sat there drinking and laughing across the sofas at each other. At some point, I felt Anthony slip his arm around my shoulders, and my skin prickled under his touch. And later, when the others had gone into the kitchen to get another round of drinks, I looked up at him, and he looked down at me, and suddenly I was lost inside his kiss and we broke off, laughing, just in time for the others to catch us.

And that was it, my first date with Anthony Riley, if you can call it a date because it all felt pretty casual right from the start.

Scotty wasn't drinking so he offered to drop us girls home that night, and back in my bedroom, as I took my make-up off before bed, I got a text message from Anthony.

Really nice seeing you, we
should do it again some
time.

I texted Remi and Jade.

But why didn't he suggest
when?! xx

Adele!! Stop worrying! xxx

A few days later, Amie and I finished college and headed back to mine together. She'd been texting Scotty for the last few days, and we had a plan to see the boys.

We did our make-up together at my house and I packed an overnight bag.

'I'm staying at Amie's tonight,' I told Mum. 'Would you give us a lift?'

Amie lived just a short walk from the big Tesco's in town, so Mum always dropped us there and did a bit of shopping while we headed down the alleyway that linked Amie's road with the supermarket. There, Amie changed her clothes and packed an overnight bag.

'I'm staying at Adele's tonight,' she told her mum. 'Her mum's waiting for us at Tesco's.'

'OK, girls,' she said.

But of course, by the time we'd headed back through the alleyway, congratulating ourselves on how well our plan had worked, it wasn't my mum who was waiting for us in her car, it was Scotty and Anthony in the green Punto.

'All right girls!' they said, grinning as they spotted our overnight bags.

The texts between me and Anthony had got cheekier and naughtier over the last few days and it was obvious we were going to have sex that night. We had a laugh that evening, sitting in Scotty's living room, drinking and joking together. His mum came home while we were watching *I'm a Celebrity … Get Me Out of Here!*

'All right Scotty,' she said, poking her head around the door. 'I'm going to bed. Don't make too much noise.'

'OK, Mum,' he said, and the night was ours.

We stayed up until the early hours, listening to music, and then finally it was time to go to bed. Amie went upstairs to Scotty's room, while I followed Anthony up to the spare room where he was sleeping.

'Sshh,' I giggled as he took off my top, and kissed me. That was the first night we slept together, and it was everything I hoped it would be. But it was, after all, just sex. Anthony made that clear from the start, and I liked him so much that I wasn't going to disagree. Like many girls, I guess, I thought that if we slept together long enough, if he got to know me, then it might change some day. For now, I was just happy that he was mine, even if it was just for a few hours a couple of times a week.

And that's how it started. Perhaps you could call us friends with benefits, and it was fun, especially as Amie was hooking up with Scotty too. It was the four of us together. Amie and I would go off to college together in the morning, and then we'd take our homework round to the boys' house and lie on the bed in Scotty's bedroom as we pored through our books and drank and joked and the boys played *Call of Duty* on the Xbox. Then, when it was time for bed, me and Anthony would go to his room and Amie would stay with Scotty. And outside of our little foursome, nobody knew what was happening, and that gave everything an added frisson. Sometimes I'd be laying in bed with Anthony in the morning and my brother Scott would text or call him.

'Why don't you tell him you're with his sister?' I'd whisper, and he'd shake his head.

'No way,' he said. 'It's not like it's anything serious. Why should anyone know?'

And I'd try to swallow down the disappointment that collected in my throat each time he said something like that. Instead I'd laugh and say 'I know' or anything else that might convince him that I wasn't taking it seriously either.

But then once a week became twice a week, and twice a week became Anthony texting and asking if we could see each other alone. Sometimes it wasn't even about the sex, we'd just cuddle up with a DVD. It was more like a relationship, and yet at the same time Anthony was always keen to let me know he was sleeping with other girls.

'I got in such a mess at the weekend, I woke up next to this ginger girl on Sunday morning,' he told me once, and I tried to laugh it off, or hit him playfully, or act like it didn't matter, but deep down, it did. Deep down maybe I wondered why I wasn't enough for him to stop seeing other girls, and it didn't matter how much fun we had together, he always left me wanting more, because come the weekend, when he was out clubbing and I knew I'd never get in at 16, I had no idea what he was doing. And then again, he wasn't shy to tell me who he'd got off with, or who he'd woken up with. But even if I didn't know it then, it was eating away at me.

Yet, at the same time, he was getting closer to me. He started staying at his dad's more, which was on my side of town so it was easier to see each other. I'd go in the house and straight upstairs, never saying hello to his dad or his step-mum, who was eight months pregnant at the time. We'd watch DVDs up in his room and when we were hungry he'd leave me there and go and get us a KFC. But we still were only friends with benefits.

We'd been like this for a couple of months when I started going to the same clubs as him. I'd be there with the girls, he'd be there with the lads – sometimes my brother among them – but we'd never speak. All of my friends knew what was going on, of course, but none of his did. Instead I'd watch from across the bar as he chatted to other girls in front of me.

'Doesn't it bother you?' my friends asked.

'But I'm the one who's going home with him,' I said.

Because when he was ready to leave I'd feel my phone buzz in my pocket and it would be a message from him.

I'm going, you coming?

I'd look up and he'd be watching me, and I'd nod and meet him out the front of the club. There was a bit of a buzz about our secrecy, something about it that made my tummy flip in excitement when my brother watched me leave the club with-out any idea that I was going home with his friend. But there was also something else swelling inside my belly, a dark feel-ing that felt like jealousy, and I was trying very hard to keep it inside and not let it come spilling out.

As much as I enjoyed the thrill of Anthony being mine and no one knowing, I was starting to wonder why he refused to tell anyone. Was he ashamed of me? Why was I his dirty little secret when he was texting me all the time, asking to see me and staying at his dad's just so we could see each other more? What was it about me that wasn't good enough for him to want to make me his girfriend? Although I tried to be casual, to go along with the rules that he'd set for our relationship, it was starting to bite deep inside. I wanted Anthony and I wanted him to want me.

And then on Christmas Eve it finally came to a head. We were out in a club, and as usual I watched from the other side of the dance floor as he danced with other girls in front of me, and then – right there, while I was watching – he started kissing one. My friends looked at me, and there was nothing I could do to keep my feelings from spilling out. Perhaps it was the vodka sloshing around in my belly, or maybe I'd just had enough. But when we bumped into each other in the club's toilets, I went mad. I was pushing him and kicking him, and although all he had to do was keep me at arm's length and I couldn't even feel my body impact with his, he must have seen how upset I was.

'How could you do this to me?' I shouted at him, losing every ounce of cool I'd worked so hard to maintain.

And then I left. Angry, humiliated, mascara running down my cheeks. The clock had already struck midnight, but it was anything but a Happy Christmas.

We didn't see each other on Christmas Day, and he hadn't bought me a present either. We texted throughout the day, and I think I realised then just how much I really liked him. But I felt like a fool too because, while I'd silently been falling for him, he'd been taking the mickey out of me by sleeping with other girls behind my back, and then, of course, flaunting it in front of my face. It was impossible to not feel completely hurt, and totally humiliated.

On Boxing Day Mum and Dad went out for the night, and Amie came round. It was Christmas and we were bored, I wanted to drown my sorrows and there was a bottle of Jägermeister in the fridge. Somehow between the first shot and the sixth we'd started messaging Scott's friends on MSN, and before we knew it, high on Jägermeister, we'd invited two of them over.

One of them was Bruce, who was dark, handsome and really fit, the one that all my friends fancied, and when he showed me attention that day, perhaps it was just what I needed. So when he tried to kiss me I pushed all thoughts of Anthony from my mind. I let myself fall into him, telling myself that this after all is what Anthony does, that he's not thinking of me when he's with other women, that perhaps I should try and behave like he does, that I should sleep with another guy. After all, like Anthony told me a dozen times, it was only a bit of fun.

And so I did, buoyed up by alcohol and immediately afterwards came down with a heavy shot of regret.

'Let's go out,' the boys said.

And because it was Christmas, and because I was drunk and because I didn't care any more, I decided to do just that, and guess who we bumped into – Anthony.

Not that he spoke to me. He did his usual thing of pretending I wasn't there, which mixed and curdled with the Jägermeister in my stomach and made me feel worthless. So maybe when he texted me asking if I was ready to go, I wanted him to feel just a little of what I did. We started arguing on the way home, I can't even remember what about, something and nothing, and so when we got back to his and we were still arguing, that's when I decided to say it, to tell him, just like he'd told me.

'We don't have to have sex anyway,' I said. 'Because I've already had some tonight.'

His face darkened, right there in front of me a shadow passed across his eyes, an unmistakable look of anger furrowed his brow. He was speechless. Gone was the petty irritation of whatever it was that we were arguing about, and in its place was a blackness I'd never seen in him before.

'What's wrong?' I said. 'You do it openly, you *tell* me.'

I sat down on the bed and stared at him.

'You're treating me like a dickhead,' I said. 'You've done the same and now I've done it, you're going to kick –'

But I didn't get chance to finish my sentence because he grabbed me by my hand and pulled me from the bed.

When he finally spoke it wasn't in his usual tone, it was in a hard, cold voice that I hadn't heard before, and made my insides turn icy cold. And those green eyes, they weren't twinkling any more. They were hard; they were frightening.

'I've got feelings for you and you've ruined it all,' he spat.

It was the first time he'd ever acknowledged he felt anything for me, and any other time I would have felt so happy, but he was dragging me from his room, pushing me down the stairs, trying to get me out of his house.

'What the hell are you doing?' I shouted. 'I'm going home!'

I opened the front door and felt a blast of freezing cold air whoosh into the house from the street. I ran out, leaving the door open behind me, but I hadn't got many steps down the road when I felt someone's arm on mine. It was his stepmum.

She was standing there in her nightie, her huge, swollen, pregnant belly wrapped in her arms.

'It's five o'clock in the morning, Adele. What's going on?'

It was the first time I'd ever spoken to her, and I felt terrible that we'd woken his parents up by arguing, but she insisted I couldn't walk home. She led me back into the house and upstairs to Anthony's room. He was sitting on his bed, his head in his hands. In this room there were two double beds, one by the window, one by the wall.

'You sleep in this one,' she said, indicating the one by the wall. 'And Anthony can sleep over by the window, and you can sort this out tomorrow when you've both calmed down.'

I must have fallen into a drunken sleep because the following morning I woke up to feel Anthony's arms around me.

'I was too cold over by the window,' he said when I stirred.

In the light of a new day, I felt absolutely terrible for what I'd done. I buried my face in my hands and wondered how on earth I could salvage whatever it was that we had. I knew I'd hurt Anthony, and I didn't want to do that, I just didn't want him to keep on hurting me.

'It wasn't true, Anthony,' I tried. 'I didn't do it. It's you that I want. I only said it because I was drunk.'

Yes, I was lying, but I just kept thinking back to what he'd said the night before, about having feelings for me, about how I'd ruined everything. I'd had no idea.

'You saying that made me realise that I don't want anyone else to have you,' he said. 'It made me realise I want you to be my girlfriend.'

And despite everything that had happened – the argument, his pulling me from the bed, practically throwing me out of the house – just hearing that from him meant everything. After all these months, after telling me that it was just a bit of fun, he did want me and I was so happy.

I snuggled down further inside his arms then, wrapped up safe in a place that I never wanted to leave.

'I won't sleep with anyone else and I don't want you to either,' he said. 'I don't want you texting boys any more.'

I did wonder why he'd said that bit. I didn't feel the need to say the same to him because I trusted him. It didn't bother me if he was texting girls because he was mine. But I nodded and agreed because right then, right at that moment, I didn't want anything to spoil what we now had. Anthony was finally my boyfriend and I'd never felt so happy.

We spent the next few days together, and would get the train to Norwich to go to the cinema, or for a meal.

'Why don't we just go out in Lowestoft?' I asked.

'It's better in Norwich,' he said. 'No one knows us there.'

'But we don't need to hide our relationship from anyone now,' I told him. 'You've got to tell my brother. It's New Year's Eve in a few days. The new year is a new start for us. You need to tell him by then, Anthony.'

He nodded, although he seemed unsure. But I was adamant.

'New year, new start,' I reminded him.

I got ready for New Year's Eve at home, slipping on a new blue dress I'd bought from New Look with a matching blue hairband to put in my backcombed hair. I painted my finger-nails and toenails black to match my shoes.

'You look nice,' Mum said when I went downstairs.

'Can I have a lift to Amie's, Mum?' I asked. 'She's having a party.'

'Yes, of course,' she said.

And then Scott appeared. 'Can I have a lift too?' he said.

We got into the car and Mum asked us both where we were going. Scott answered first.

'I'm off out with your boyfriend,' he said.

It felt odd hearing it from him, but in a good way because I knew then Anthony had done it.

'What boyfriend?' Mum said.

'His name's Anthony,' I said. 'He's 19, the same as Scott.'

'Oh, I need to meet him,' Mum replied.

Just seconds after Scott got out of the car, a text came through on my phone from Anthony.

I've told your brother, he
seems ok. xx

I smiled. So that was it now, no more sneaking around, we were a proper couple.

We had a few drinks at Amie's that night before heading to a pub to meet all the boys. Anthony was there, and this time I didn't need to worry about going over and saying hello. In fact, he came over to me. And then before we knew it the countdown to the new year had begun.

'Five ... four ... three ... two ... one ... Happy New Year!' everyone cried.

But in among the poppers going off and people hugging and kissing and singing 'Auld Lang Syne', Anthony pulled me out of the back of the pub. There he held my hands and looked at me so seriously.

'Please promise me something,' he said. 'Promise me you'll always be there for me. You're the only girl I've ever felt like this about, but you've got to promise you'll always be there for me because I'm not the person you think I am.'

I stared deep into his green eyes; he was serious. But I was drunk and fireworks were shooting into the black sky around me, so I just wrapped him up in a hug and told him what he wanted me to say.

'Of course I'll always be there for you, Anthony,' I said. And then we hugged and kissed because it was New Year's Eve and what else do you do?

It kept coming back to me though, every few days, what Anthony had said, those eight words: I'm not the person you think I am. What did he mean? Not that I asked him, I assumed that he, like me, was just drunk and emotional. So I tried to push it to the back of my mind, told myself it didn't mean anything.

Anyway, after New Year's Eve we were pretty much inseparable, or at least that's how Anthony seemed to want it to be, we both did. Once everybody knew about us there was no reason to hide or sneak around, or pretend we didn't want to see each other. So we saw as much of each other as we could, and I was so happy.

I started back at college a few days into the new year and Anthony would text me through my classes.

'Is that him again?' my friends would say. 'He must *really* like you.'

He'd even come and meet me on my breaks, and at lunch he'd take me out to lunch, or back to Scotty's where he rustled up beans on toast or sausage and chips. The girls were always so impressed, after all, having an older boyfriend to take you out for lunch seemed so much more grown up than any of the boys they were seeing. And that made me feel special, important.

At the end of the day, as me and Amie filtered from class, he'd be there to walk me home.

Wednesday was my day off and the two of us loved nothing better than just enjoying a lazy morning in bed together. One day, as we lay there, I traced my fingers along his tattoos.

'What's this one?' I asked, stroking one on the top of his right arm. It was a cross with a name written underneath it: 'Margaret'.

'It's my mum,' he said gently, tracing his own finger across the name. 'She died when I was 15.'

His words hung in the air between us as my mind scrambled for something to say. But what can you say to that? Instead I wrapped my arms around his waist and snuggled into his chest. Perhaps sometimes you don't need any words.

We'd have fun on those Wednesdays too. Mum had bought me a wax pot for Christmas as she knew it would come in handy for my beauty course, but I decided to try it out on Anthony first.

'Ooh!' he said, wriggling as I smeared the warm wax onto his chest with a spatula.

'Hold still,' I replied. 'Otherwise it's going to really hurt.'

'I still can't believe you convinced me to do this,' he said. 'Why can't you practise another massage on me?'

'No pain, no gain,' I laughed. 'Ready?'

He nodded, and with one big pull I pulled his hair off his chest with the cloth.

'Ouch!' he cried. And I laughed and laughed, and finally after rubbing his chest he did too.

The Anthony who let me paint face masks on his cheeks and dab cream under his eyes was a world away from the man everyone else knew, and that made our relationship feel all the more special. He didn't care when his mates were moaning that he spent too much time with me, instead he sent their calls to voicemail and snuggled up on his dad's sofa with me watching another DVD.

He looked after me too. I only had to mention that I fancied a Ribena and he'd be down the shop getting me one. Or he'd be up and down the stairs to his bedroom, making me a cup of tea or a slice of toast, and it felt nice to be looked after. I felt safe with Anthony. But it wasn't like I hadn't seen that he had an edge, with other people, of course, not me. When he got drunk he would get a bit angry: it was almost like he was looking for a fight with people at the bar. But I'd pull on his arm, and whisper to him to go home, and he was fine. Because under that hard exterior, I knew Anthony was a softie. I liked the fact that people referred to me as 'Anthony's girlfriend'. While I was with him I'd never have any boys hassling me, that was for sure.

We went from 0 to 60 in a matter of days. There was rarely a morning when I wouldn't wake up to a text message from him. He'd take me on the train to Norwich to go to the cinema, or for a meal, and he always picked up the bill.

'You're so lucky,' Amie would tell me. And I knew I was. Having Anthony to myself was all I'd ever wanted, and he was the perfect boyfriend, so charming, so wonderful. I could feel myself falling for him. Not that Mum thought he was as wonderful as me. She met him a few days into the new year when some of Scott's friends were over at my house drinking. Anthony came over to meet them and it seemed like the best time to introduce him to my parents.

He shook their hands and said all the right things, and as I went to leave to go out with them, Mum called to him: 'Make sure you look after her.'

'Don't worry, I will,' he said.

But the next day when I asked her what she thought of him, she pulled a face.

'I don't know,' she said. 'There's just something about him.'

But she didn't know Anthony like I did. No one did.

In mid-January he'd planned a Thursday night out with the lads. I decided not to go because I had college the next day, but I texted him while he was out.

Have a good night xx

Thanks babe xx

But the next morning I didn't wake up to a message from him like I usually did. Instead there was one from his friend Chris saying: Call me.

First I tried Anthony's phone, but it just went to voicemail, and then I assumed maybe he was using Chris's phone, so I called. But when Chris answered and I asked for Anthony, I was unprepared for his reply.

'He got arrested last night,' he said.

'Arrested!'

'Yeah, he had a fight. They've remanded him in custody.'

'Remanded him? What? Why?'

'Well, he's only been out of prison a few months, hasn't he?'

I let the words settle a moment. Prison? Anthony? This was the first I'd heard. And in that second, with those few words, everything came crashing down. My happiness plummeted through the roof, landing in a pile at my feet. I'd never even known anyone who'd been arrested, let alone gone to prison. And now I was being told that person was my boyfriend.

'He's not in court until Monday ...' Chris was saying. 'We'll know more then ...'

But when I put the phone down I couldn't stop the tears. Monday? So I had to spend the whole weekend without him.

I staggered downstairs to Mum, my tears already streaking long salty trails down my cheeks.

'Oh Adele,' she said, wrapping me in a hug as I cried to her. 'You're too young for all this, you don't need to get involved with a lad like this.'

'But I really like him, Mum,' I sobbed. 'I really *really* like him. It's such a downer to start the new year like this.'

I was absolutely devastated, but then my phone rang. It was Anthony.

'Babe, I'm so so sorry,' he said. 'I'm only allowed one phone call but I had to ring you.'

'What happened?' I sobbed.

'I was in this club and someone slagged my mum off and I beat him up.'

'Oh Anthony,' I said.

I felt torn then because instantly I could imagine how he might have felt. I remembered how quiet he'd been when he told me about his mum dying, how all I could do was wrap him up in my arms. I knew too how angry he got when he was drunk and I hated myself for not being there, because I would have been able to stop him and then we wouldn't have been in this mess.

'I know, I know, I'm sorry, but you promised me you'd wait for me.'

'Of course but why –'

'Just keep your promise,' he said. And then he was gone.

Without Anthony's arms to comfort me, I fell into my mum's.

'You can understand why he did it,' I said.

'It's terrible,' she said. 'But he should have thought of you, he should have walked away. Don't get mixed up in all this, Adele, you're too young.'

But didn't she see? I already was.

CHAPTER 2

CONTROL

For the next 24 hours my mind veered wildly one way and then the other. Sometimes I felt angry when I remembered this wasn't Anthony's first stint in prison, a detail that when we'd been lying in bed, a tangle of arms and legs, he'd conveniently forgotten to tell me. It certainly explained why I'd never seen him around before that September when we'd met. And that made me feel angry, especially when I thought back to that conversation as the clock struck 12 on New Year's Eve – among the fireworks and happiness those eight words from him: *'I'm not the man you think I am.'* Was this what he meant?

My phone didn't stop that day, not once word had got round about the fight. Apparently Anthony had broken the guy's arm and his jaw, though of course Chinese whispers over the weekend exaggerated his injuries more and more. But everybody thought that the only person who really knew was me, and so that's why they were calling and texting. It was big news among our crowd, and I was at the centre of it, which, I'll admit, at 16 felt exciting.

What's happened to
Anthony?

Heard Anthony's in jail. U
ok, hun? x

And yet the irony was I felt completely in the dark. After all, it turned out I didn't really know my boyfriend at all. And that made the anger boil and bubble inside.

In the next moment, though, I felt overwhelmingly sorry for him. I closed my eyes and all I could picture was that tattoo on his right arm, that tribute to his dead mum. Who wouldn't flip if someone said something about her? Someone he'd loved so much that he chose to carry her in black ink at his side always. Wouldn't anyone do the same?

'You can't wait for him, Adele,' Mum said. 'You don't want to get mixed up in all that, you've got the rest of your life ahead of you.'

Dad glanced up from the TV. 'Your mum said she knew something wasn't right about him,' he offered.

But I heard myself saying a spiel that would become so familiar to me over the coming days and weeks, it was me defending him, it was me telling everyone that they didn't know him like me. 'Imagine if your mum had died, wouldn't you flip if someone was slagging her off?' I asked whoever would listen.

And what could people say? Although deep down, maybe it wasn't about what they thought, maybe it was me convincing myself.

But despite everything, I missed him. That weekend I felt so cold and alone in my bed at night. I wanted to be able to turn over and snuggle into his arms, or reach out and feel the warmth of him. I wanted us to wake up and giggle about something silly that had happened the night before, or to beg him to fetch me a cup of tea in the morning before I'd even properly opened my eyes.

I missed him so much that on Monday morning I woke up and decided that I would go to court and see him. Not that I told Mum. I got dressed for college that day in my black tunic with the diamante collar so I wouldn't rouse any suspicions, then I called in sick and headed to Lowestoft Combined Court. The building with its long, sloping brown roof and green tinted windows felt so alien and imposing to me, I'd never even been inside a court before. A week ago I was enjoying the first flushes of a new relationship – my first proper relationship – and now I was here, and somewhere inside that building my boyfriend was behind bars.

I passed through the entrance doors and security checks and towards the courtroom where Anthony's hearing was going to take place. There, outside, I recognised some of his family: his dad, his stepmum, his aunties and even a cousin. And then it twisted inside me again, ever so faintly, that feeling of anger towards Anthony. I shouldn't be meeting his extended family for the first time like this. He should be here with me, introducing me to people. It was his fault that I was having to go through this, it wasn't meant to be like this. But then again, a few minutes later, as we filed silently into court and I saw him standing there inside the glass-panelled dock, I felt the familiarity of him pull at my insides, I wanted to be inside those arms, not trapped away from them in the public gallery.

He looked over, blowing me a kiss, but my nerves only offered him a tight smile and a wave in return.

The hearing began, though I couldn't understand much of what the lawyers were saying. It all felt so foreign to me, and Anthony hardly spoke, only to confirm his name and his address. Before I knew it, though, it was over, and they were taking him out of the door at the back of the dock.

'Where are they taking him?' I quickly asked his dad.

'Back to prison,' he sighed. 'He's got to serve the rest of his previous sentence.'

'What? How long is that?' I said, panicked.

'Seven months.'

And then the world started to spin. Seven months? Seven months of not seeing Anthony?

I left the court in a daze, texting my friends as tears blurred the screen in my hand.

Anthony's got seven
months :-(xx

At home, Mum dried my tears.

'You can't wait on him, Adele,' she said. 'Don't waste your life on him.'

'But I really like him, Mum.'

She sighed.

'Well, if he likes you, when he comes out you can be together.'

But what about the promise I'd made to him? And anyway, I *wanted* to wait for him. Anthony had changed my life, I could be myself with him. For months I'd tried to pretend that I was happy just to be friends with benefits, but now I didn't have to act, now I didn't have to try and be someone else, someone who was cool only to meet up for sex, because I liked being 'Anthony's girlfriend', I liked other people knowing I was 'Anthony's girlfriend'. That made me feel special, *he* made me feel special, and attractive, and wanted, and important, and … well, someone. Each day when he'd been there waiting for me to come out of college, I'd felt all of those things as my friends watched me leave hand-in-hand with him. *My* boyfriend, *my* Anthony, someone everyone had heard of, and that in itself made *me* feel like someone. I would wait six months to feel like that again if I had to, I vowed to myself.

Anthony rang me that afternoon.

'Seven months, Anthony!' I cried to him.

'Don't worry, babe,' he said. 'I'm going to appeal, I'll be out in a few weeks.'

He sounded so confident, I knew I had no reason to doubt him.

'It'll be fine. Just promise you'll wait for me.'

'Of course I will,' I said, as tears ran down my cheeks.

But Mum was right: at 16, seven months felt like a lifetime.

A few nights later a number came up on my phone that I didn't recognise. It was a mobile number.

'Hello?'

'Adele, it's me!'

'Anthony!'

Somehow, despite being in prison, he'd managed to get hold of a mobile phone.

'Are you allowed to have them?' I asked.

'No!' he said. 'I've got to make sure they don't catch me.'

'But then how –'

'Don't worry about it,' he said. 'It happens here, they throw them over the fence. As long as no one finds out you're fine.'

I sighed. What did I know about prison life? Having a boyfriend in jail was all new to me, and now I was so worried about Anthony getting in even more trouble if he got caught. But I couldn't deny the other part of me that was just so excited to pick up the phone and hear his voice. A phone call that wouldn't be cut short by the beeps down the prison line.

'We can text each other whenever we want now,' he said. 'We can speak every evening. I did this for you, Adele, because I can't stand being away from you.'

And although I hated the idea of him taking risks, my heart swelled with flattery.

'Oh Anthony, I miss you so much.'

We chatted for two hours, it was amazing, like he wasn't even stuck away in prison, locked up each night, but like he was just around the corner at his dad's or at Scotty's. I knew he was risking everything just to be able to talk to me, but it felt worth it because suddenly I didn't feel so alone any more. I'd got used to having him around, of seeing his face, of him being there when I came out of college, or to take me for lunch, and even though it hadn't even been a week I missed him so much. But this, this made all the difference.

Most week nights I'd finish college and go straight home rather than to Amie's or Rachel's house. I'd stay in, doing my beauty coursework, my phone next to me as I wrote up my assignments, waiting for the moment when he'd call and I could lie back on my bed and speak to the man I loved, locked up in a cell 30 miles away from me in Norwich Prison.

When it came to the weekends, I'd douse myself in Calvin Klein perfume, I'd slick on lipstick and fake eyelashes, but as I stared at my reflection, all glammed up ready to go out, I'd sigh. It didn't feel right without Anthony. A text on my phone would shake me out of my sigh.

Just got on the bus x

Amie.

My cue to leave the house. I'd grab my bag and most importantly my phone, and I'd head out the door.

I did still enjoy going out with the girls, but I always kept one eye on my phone in case Anthony called. Once he did, I'd leave them in the pub and stand outside, even if it was raining, just for the chance to talk to him. Outside with the smokers, I might spot one of Anthony's mates, and before I had a chance to stop them they'd grab the phone off me.

'Riley! All right mate?' one would say, sucking on a cigarette and wandering a few feet away with my phone.

I felt good that even from this pub, and him locked away in that cell, he could still chat to his friends. I thought he'd be buzzing when they finally handed the phone back to me, but the irritation in his voice was instant.

'Are you talking to boys out there?' he'd say.

'No!' I promised him. 'I'm out with the girls, and I just saw your mates and thought you'd want to say hello –'

'I don't want you talking to boys. I don't even know why you're out when I'm stuck in here.'

'Anthony, I –'

But then the phone went dead, and so too then did the rest of my night. I spent the little time we had left before drinking-up time trying to call him back, or text him, but he never answered.

'I'm gonna go home,' I told the girls.

'Oh Adele, don't go, stay out with us.'

But it didn't feel right any more, and if I'm honest the guilt was starting to bite at my insides. In the taxi home alone, my finger repeatedly dialled Anthony's mobile without luck. He'd obviously switched his phone off. But each time I tried to call, it just hit me more – him locked up there, us all out in our usual haunts, was it any wonder that he found it hard to listen to us having fun? I got home and took my make-up off, slipping into my bed, tucked up in my cosy duvet, the last of the night out still ringing in my ears. Here I was, free to come and go, while he was having to sleep in his cell. I would try harder to make it easier for him to be away, there must be more that I could do. I couldn't stand the thought of upsetting him, or us arguing, or me feeling like this when I couldn't get hold of him. I wouldn't be able to live like this for the next seven months, neither of us could …

The following morning, I was so relieved to wake up to a text from him.

Morning baby, sorry about
last night, it's just hard
being locked up when I
want to be out there with
you x

As I lay in my bed, reading over all our old texts, my stomach fizzing at the thought of him, I felt on top of the world that everything was OK again. When it was just the two of us – me in my bedroom, him in his cell – he wasn't annoyed with me, he wasn't short-tempered. That's what we needed to hang on to, those were the times that were the most valuable now.

The weeks went by like that. He'd text me to hurry home from my friend's house so that we could lie in our beds, 30 miles away from each other, and talk about anything we wanted. We both started opening up, our relationship became deeper, more intimate, even though I missed so desperately the feel of his skin against mine. Perhaps because of the distance, and not only despite it, we became closer and closer, and that was worth rushing home for. I told Anthony things about myself, my fears, my worries that I hadn't told anyone, and he opened up to me about his life, about his family, about his mum.

'What happened to her, Anthony?' I asked one night. I obviously knew she'd died, but I had no idea how.

There was silence from the other end of the phone, just for a second, and then a quiet voice said, 'She committed suicide.'

'Oh Anthony,' I said, my heart wanting to reach all the way from Lowestoft to Norwich and wrap him up in my arms.

He told me how his parents had split up and he'd been living up in Scotland with his mum. He'd come down to stay with his dad for the summer holidays, and just before he did, he'd had a massive row with his mum, telling her he was moving to live with his dad.

'My sister found her ...' he said.

His voice trailed off. I thought of my own mum downstairs watching telly while I chatted on the phone in my room. How on earth I'd feel if one day she just wasn't there any more in the spot I knew she'd always be.

'I can't imagine what you've been through,' I told him.

'I try not to think about it,' he said. 'But it's why I get angry when I drink because I think of Mum, because I argued with her before she died.'

He told me that his mum had suffered from postnatal depression when he was born, so he'd lived with his aunt until he was three, despite the fact that he had two older sisters and a brother.

'I've never let anyone get close to me before because I always thought they'd let me down,' he said. 'Not until you ...'

'I won't let you down,' I said.

'You promised that on New Year's Eve.'

'I know, I meant it. We can be happy when you get out, you'll see.'

When we hung up that night I lay in my bedroom and thought of everything Anthony had been through. I could change him, I was sure of it. I could make him see that not everyone would let him down, not everyone he loved would leave. I'd stick around, I'd prove to him that he was worth hanging around for, and then we'd put all of this behind us, because I knew the real Anthony, the sensitive Anthony, the one that no one else did.

Those stolen phone calls became my life, and the nights out somehow became less important, or at least less important than speaking to Anthony on the phone. I could hear in his voice how much it upset him to ring me and hear that I was out having fun. He didn't mean to shout, or put the phone down, it was just how he dealt with the unfairness of it all. I understood that. The arguments that followed made the nights out less fun anyway. They weren't worth it if they were going to upset him and leave us rowing. So as the weeks went by, I just decided to stay in a bit more, give Anthony less to worry about – it became easier that way. It made sense.

Friends would text:

Fancy coming out tonight?

No, Anthony might call. xx

My friends understood. They never pushed me.

He still called me from the prison phone once a day too, so as not to arouse any suspicion that he was speaking to me any other way. He wrote me letters too. I'd come home from college during the tail end of the wet, cold winter, streets lit by lamps at 4 pm, the hope of spring feeling like a million years away, and mum would nod towards the kitchen worktop.

'Another letter's arrived for you from the prison,' she'd say.

And an envelope would be laying there addressed to me with that same familiar handwriting.

A bit of lightness on a dark day.

I'd race up to my bedroom and tear it open, laying back on my bed to take in every detail of it:

I think about you all the time. The boy next to me was playing that 'Sex on Fire' song the other day and I had to tell him to turn it off because it just reminded me of when I first met you round Scotty's. It really does hurt how much I miss you and miss all the stuff we used to do. I keep hoping I'll wake up in the morning and it was all just a big dream and I was at home with you.

I'd hold the letter close and smile. Those were the things that made the days seem brighter, and each one not so long after all. This made the days feel warmer, or made me seek out the blue sky behind the clouds on a drizzly day. And it made the weeks pass much more quickly. At night we'd chat for hours once he was in his cell and no one knew he was on a mobile phone to me, and Anthony was happier, much happier than when he was ringing me and I was out in the pub. So I stopped dousing myself in Calvin Klein perfume and putting on thick black mascara, I was in my pyjamas with a cup of tea, watching *Britain's Got Talent* on the sofa with Mum and Dad and waiting for Anthony to call.

'You not going out tonight, Adele?' Dad would ask.

'Nah,' I'd say. 'Don't fancy it.'

And I saw them pass a look between them, because it must have been obvious I was waiting for Anthony to call. Mum had never liked the fact I was out too much anyway – at least this way I was concentrating on my college work; perhaps they just wished it wasn't to wait for a boy in prison. Not that they said anything to me, I was nearly 17, they knew they couldn't tell me what to do anyway.

I knew they didn't want me visiting Anthony in prison, though, that much they'd made clear.

'We didn't bring you up like that, Adele,' Mum had warned me.

At 16 I was never going to be allowed into the prison on my own, I had to be with someone over 18, and Mum and Dad weren't going to take me, so Anthony arranged that his dad and stepmum would give me a lift.

Two weeks later I found myself squashed into the back of their black Lexus car, alongside the new baby, as we made polite conversation. I'd bought a new outfit especially, some new jeans and a pretty top. I'd spent longer than usual doing my make-up, but when I arrived at those imposing red brick prison gates, I suddenly felt so out of place, so overdressed, so intimidated.

'Just follow us,' Anthony's dad said casually.

The huge gates opened and we were shepherded inside. I looked around at the other people who were waiting, their scruffy clothes, their tattoos, and I wished that I'd worn a little less lip gloss, that the top I was wearing covered me up a little more. They looked me up and down in a way that told me they knew it was my first time, and I shifted uncomfortably inside my jacket. I felt Anthony's dad's hand on my shoulder.

'He's going to be so thrilled to see you,' he said.

I managed a smile in return, telling myself as I looked round at the hard black metal of the guns that the prison officers were carrying, at the cold expression that matched each of their faces as they checked one after the other of us off a list, that this was all for Anthony. I scanned the rest of the visitors we were waiting with, my eyes falling on one woman in particular. Unlike me she hadn't dressed up especially: from the looks of things she hadn't even put a comb through her hair; she bounced a screaming toddler on her hip, sighing each time we were ushered into a different room as if she were doing nothing more unusual than waiting in line in a supermarket for a particularly slow cashier. I doubted that this would ever become so normalised for me. At least I only had seven months to wait – these women looked like they'd been waiting a lifetime.

We stepped up to a desk and were ticked off a sheet and in exchange for our names we were given a number and herded through the prison gates into a separate room where we handed over our identification and the door was locked behind us. The echo of it rattled around the room, and I tried to still my racing heart, without luck. We were then led into a pen, before the door behind us was locked and then another room unlocked, and then – Anthony's dad told me – we were finally inside the prison. There we were searched by sniffer dogs, and we walked through an electrical security arch, much like those you see in airports. Once through that we were searched again, the prison officer asking me to slip off my jacket, and standing there, the thin straps of my top expos-ing my shoulders to the cold, I just wanted to close my eyes and pretend I was anywhere else but there. But then again, I told myself again, this experience, this humiliation, it was all for Anthony.

We went up to another desk and told the officer there who we were seeing. We were given a number for the table we were to sit at and slowly I made my way across the room, my eyes catching sight of the prisoners in their orange and yellow hi-vis bibs already sat with their loved ones, and the guards dotted around the room, one hand on the guns that hung across their chests. And then I heard one of the officers call out Anthony's name, and before I knew it he was walking over to our table, not in the frightened way I had shuffled in, but striding towards us confidently, like this was home, a smile plastered wide across his face.

'All right, son,' his dad said, getting up and giving him a brief pat on his back.

Anthony looked at me. 'Well, aren't you going to give me a hug, baby?'

I glanced around at the prison officers.

'It's OK,' Anthony laughed. 'I won't bite!'

And he and his dad laughed. 'She's had that same look on her since we got here,' his dad told him. I shuffled in my seat, realising that the fear I felt inside must have found its way onto my face that whole time.

'That's OK, baby,' Anthony said. 'Nice girl like you doesn't belong somewhere like here.'

I felt my chest swell then because Anthony understood me; he knew what I was thinking all along. I got up and put my arms around him, keeping my eye on the guards the whole time.

I was excited to see Anthony. I'd missed the feel of him so much, but not like this. While Anthony chatted to his dad, I looked around the room, spotting the woman and the toddler

I'd seen earlier. She was arguing with the man I presumed was her husband while their little boy played at their feet.

After about 20 minutes, Anthony's dad left. I got up to go with him, but he signalled for me to stay.

'I'll get off, leave you two lovebirds in peace.'

'All right Dad, see ya,' Anthony said, as his dad explained where he'd be waiting for me outside.

I nodded, and once he'd gone, when it was just me and Anthony for the first time, and it was only his eyes I had to focus on, I felt myself relax just a little.

'You look gorgeous, babe,' he said.

I looked around the room and felt myself blush.

'Hey, don't worry about them, look at me,' Anthony said.

And finally sitting there, just inches away from my man, holding hands across the table and within our grasp everything that was precious about our relationship, I tried so hard to forget everything else around me. This may not have been how I had imagined the beginning of our relationship, but something inside told me – just like the woman and the screaming toddler – that it was something I was just going to have to get used to.

If I was honest, I never enjoyed those visits. I knew every time I went that my mum was right, I wasn't brought up to be visiting a boyfriend in prison. But I did it for Anthony, just like I made sure I was home after college by 8 pm so that he could call me, just like I stopped going out because I couldn't bear the endless questions the next day, or upsetting him and causing him to be in a mood if I did.

My seventeenth birthday came and went with a card from Anthony from prison – not exactly how I'd been planning on spending it, but over the last couple of months I'd learnt to rely on phone calls in place of hugs, and letters in place of meals out with my boyfriend.

Despite the distance, we got to know each other better with every phone call. There were still arguments, just like with any relationship, if I was at one of the girls' houses when he called, instead of being at home like I said I would be, or if I had a rare night out because it was someone's birthday. But the most important thing was we got over them, that I understood because of Anthony's past why he was the way he was, that he was insecure, that he thought just like everyone else that I wouldn't stick around for him. But I was proving to Anthony every single day that I meant what I said on New Year's Eve, and it was paying off.

He'd been in prison for three months when we were chatting one evening after lights out.

'I really love you, Adele,' he said suddenly.

'What?'

'I love you. No one else would have waited for me like you have.'

'Of course I'm waiting, Anthony. I said I would.'

'And that's why I love you.'

I put the phone down and was feeling all fuzzy inside, safer somehow as I wrapped my duvet up around me and drifted off to sleep, because that was the first time Anthony had said he loved me, and I realised then that I loved him too.

After that, though, time seemed to pass differently, somehow faster and slower at the same time. The letters that

Anthony sent me kept me going as tiny new green leaves slowly unfurled themselves on branches that had been stripped bare by the cold, dark months, as the light started to bleed into every afternoon, and winter finally turned to spring ...

I'm in a mess babe, I need you, I wouldn't know what to do without you, you're my world. You're the love of my life, my one and true love, I'll never ever feel this way about anyone again. I really really hope and wish I don't lose you, please please please don't be going out all the time, I don't want nothing at all coming in between us. I know I moan and shout and get pissed off it's only cos I love you so much, the last three months and for however long I've known you, you're all I've dreamed about and thought and wished for. We've been through the wars so far but we are standing strong, damn we love each other, that's not something we're going to find with anyone else. You're definitely my one in a million, nah you're my one in a trillion ...

Baby, it's now 8.30 was speaking to you earlier. I'm so so so in love with you its unbelievable, I'm so happy we're gonna be all right. Time would be so hard without you cos whenever I'm pissed off or finding it hard I think of you and I smile. You've got that charm on me, I just think of your cheeky smile and everything seems to be better. We're gonna be ok aren't we? You do love me, don't you, cheeky? Yeh, good girl. LOL. I love you so so much, 100 per cent, no 1000 per cent. LOL. You're going to be mine forever ain't you? You're gonna be my wife and we're going to have lots of little Rileys aint we? Too far LOL, nah I'm just dreaming. We'll definitely have little Rileys I'm sure of it. I can't wait to have a family with you. Babe, I'm in a mess, can't stop thinking of you, you've been on my mind constantly today, words can't describe how much I love you.

The daffodils pushed their way out of the earth, blooming bright yellow before dropping their heads, and returning to the soil, and making way for the summer flowers that shot up in bright bursts of red and gold and blue. And Anthony's letters kept on coming, shining more brightly in my life than any sunny day that the new season had to offer, my reward for waiting for him.

Hey babe, well, what a visit, made me happy, you're so beautiful, I'm glad you chose to wait on me. I'm so happy that we sorted everything out, I do trust you and believe you. When you promised not to go out made me realise you really do love me so you made me the happiest boy ever :-) least now my head ain't gonna be fucked up :-)

I promise you as well if you stick to your side of the deal I won't moan anymore cos I really want us to work. Seeing you today just made me realise even more how much you mean to me, so please don't ruin it, it's all in your hands, especially tomorrow when England play. You promised me in the letter and to my face, you let me down I swear on my mum's grave I will never go back to you if you do choose the pub over me, how could I forgive you, you wouldn't if it was me. But I know it ain't gonna come to that cos I know you love me and I'm lucky to have your support. Fuck, I need it cos this time is really killing me but won't for that long cos I'm out this year so hey, we will be back together soon, stronger than ever, if you do stand by me without going to pubs and that I will owe you the world anyways. Love you in the morning, at night, all the while, big time, millions, billions, trillions, forever and ever.

But just like with any couple we had our ups and downs. We both made mistakes. Mine always seemed to be when I had a rare night out with my friends. The next day Anthony would be really fuming.

'I've already heard from my friends,' he spat down the phone. 'They said you were talking to boys, they saw you, Adele.'

Anthony, I –'

'Don't lie to me, do you think I don't believe my mates? Why else would they tell me?'

It didn't matter how many times I told him that I wasn't, that they were making it up, that I didn't so much as look at another boy, whatever they said got stuck in Anthony's head, and he'd lose it.

'I can't deal with this, Adele. Me stuck in here and you out there talking to boys. I asked you not to go out, you promised. I can't do this any more …'

He'd dump me and hang up, and I'd pad downstairs in my slippers, hot, salty tears coursing down my cheeks, and Mum's arms to wrap me up down in the kitchen.

'It would be impossible for anyone to make a relationship like this work,' she'd say. 'You're too young for all this.'

But I'd tell her, all relationships have their ups and downs.

Well, this is a hard and awkward one, I started, well tried to start, writing this loads of times since I came off the phone to you, simply because I can't find the words. But now I had time to think about it I was right to end it now cause I told you what would happen when I lost the game and within four days it's started. It's all right you saying nah I'm not going out again til Christmas and all this but how many times you said this to me? And it's all right you saying you can trust me but no matter what or how strong anyone's relationship is when they are in jail it always casts that little bit of doubt, and the states you get yourself in it only takes one stupid little mistake and it would not only break us I would end up hating you and I don't want that.

Those letters were the hardest to read, but it never really mattered by then because usually Anthony would have rung me before the letter arrived.

'I miss you, baby, I can't live without you.'

And we'd be back together again. This became our pattern, the drama of the outside world recreated in our long-distance relationship.

Most of our memories were brilliant weren't they? It is the memories of getting to know you that I will never forget, we had some good convos even some of the little weird ones about the past ... when we use to cuddle in the middle of my room for ages ... when we was meeting up and every weekend we used to wake up and go 'not you again!' but really I liked waking up to you :-) Just stupid little things like meeting up from college, emotional little kisses in bed, cuddling up to you at night ... you are a unique beautiful one of a kind girl and anyone is lucky to have you and I am happy I really got to know you and I'm happy you were my first love and the first girl I opened up to, I feel like I can say anything to you, Cheeky ...

And another ...

All the times we had good/bad were the best time I had with any girl, I loved it all just didn't have the balls to tell you when I was out there, I had to act like hard Riley. I knew I liked you for ages, I loved all the times we met up, I used to pretend I wasnt falling for you, Scotty and Glen was saying I was cos everytime Scotty didn't really wanna meet yous but I would talk him round. I dunno what it was about you, I just wanted to see you all the time, wasn't just about the sex, there was something that made me feel weird and I liked it, that's why I was so gutted about Bruce :-(but that made me realise you was right for me and I had to get you and cut my shit out too and I did :-) thats why I kept saying you came from nowhere and stole my heart cos you took it soon as I met you that night outside the pub. The first night I slept with you at Scotty's must have done something cos I didn't want anyone after that, the people I got with after that it didn't feel the same, I didn't want it.

The seasons kept on changing, the heat of the summer faded after it had burnt the leaves on the trees into golds and browns, and still Anthony was locked away from me. He kept writing to me saying that it would be just a few more weeks, a few more weeks, but in the end I knew that it was nothing more than wishful thinking on his part. Why else would he say it?

Before long the wind had stolen the last of the leaves from the branches and Christmas lights were starting to twinkle on plastic trees tucked away behind cosy living-room windows. The letters kept on coming, some declaring Anthony's love for me, others planning what we'd do when we got out. He'd write about how we'd get a flat together and those little fantasies were what I hung on for. Others were written when he'd finished with me before taking it all back, but the ones that really broke my heart were the ones that revealed just a little more about what Anthony had been through. More than anything else, they were the ones that made me determined to stick around.

Trust me Adele, when I was 13/14 that's when my world changed, up until then I got bullied cos I was fat but soon as I realised I could fight I put it to use, found the gang, started drinking ... then in no time everyone was talking about the Riley boy. (LOL) Thats where it went wrong, it got to my head, I thought I was the daddy when I was 14. I nearly killed one of the biggest drug dealers in our area's boys with a hatchet. I only got community service and a five year suspended sentence for that, but got sent down here thank god cos most of the boys up there are dead or doing life sentences ...

What a life he had before me. No wonder he was so determined to hang on to what we have.

> I've got so much to say sorry for but I'm fed up saying sorry, it's not even about that anymore. I should not have fucked your head up, I didn't mean it, it was my sentences, I should not have allowed you to do it with me, that was unfair. I should have known this would have fucked us up, I've been in jail that long … I've seen loads of my boys crumble cos of rumours about their girlfriend while they were in jail. It wasn't good, people don't know how much jail affects people, how stuff gets in their heads, they think it's fun and games but it's hard and yes it's our faults and we shouldn't expect them to wait for us but with us it felt different, I couldn't let go, no matter how much it hurt. I should have been stronger but proves I aint as hard as people think.

We made it through 11 months like that. I'd waited that long, and finally, just before Christmas, it was about to pay off because Anthony was up for parole. And then I got the phone call from him to tell me that – once again – he'd been turned down. He was staying inside for the rest of his sentence which was another two years. Two years of my life like this, after I'd already waited this long.

'I'm so sorry, Adele,' Anthony kept saying, sobbing down the phone, and what could I say to him then?

'What am I going to do with myself now?' was all I could manage.

'You've got to move on, forget about me.'

Could I? But then I had no idea if I could keep waiting, and the alternative was breaking his heart and mine by ending our relationship. But how could I carry on like this? I was 17 years old, maybe Mum had been right. I thought back to the woman bouncing a toddler on her hip, how she'd looked so at home in that prison. Was that really going to be me after all?

Soz I hung up earlier, I didn't know what to do with myself, I'm in a mess. I can't listen to you cry, it's too emotional. I'm heartbroken, Adele, I'm not even gonna lie, I feel lost, nothing feels real.

There is so much I wanna say to you but I honestly can't find the words, I'm speechless. Nothing makes sense at the moment, my life is just one big mess, god knows where to start or how to start rebuilding it. I got 25 months to think about that one, my release date at the moment is 28th January 2012.

Earlier you said what are you supposed to do with yourself now, I can't answer that one for you Adele, but I can say you are much better off without me I'm just a pure fuck up you could do much better than some prison boy, you're a beautiful girl, hard to understand (LOL) nah, seriously, though babe you are the love of my life. I fell for you hard, I'm devastated this happened, you are my world, prison time don't bother me one bit, I'm used to it, the thing that knocked me back, took the breath away from me, is breaking your heart, telling you to move on cos it's not what I want one bit. I fucking love you more than I can say, I wish I could keep you forever, but that's wrong, the right thing is to let you go. I can't fuck up your life anymore

than I already have, you deserve so much better ... I'm so
so sorry babe and wish you all the luck in the world.

But I didn't leave him, of course I didn't. Instead he sent me a
Christmas card from prison, and we started the new year
apart.

Well not over a year yet babe, but near a year – a year
next week so by the time you get this (28th jan). But
you're right, I am your man. Yeh, I know baby we have
both got fucked up heads, mainly my fault sorry. All we
can do now is give it the best shot, and if we still fuck up it
just means we ain't ready ... but it won't come to that cos
we are a good couple and I love you very very much.

And what do you mean 'mmm, one day maybe Mrs
Adele Hillary Riley??' You will be Mrs Riley one day. I
usually get what I want and you are the only girl I want so
you're fucked (LOL) may as well admit it babe :-)

March came around and so too did my eighteenth birthday.
Anthony sent me a card from prison, but he knew I wanted to
go out to celebrate it. I got dressed up and went out with my
friends around town. It felt good to be out, to feel the alcohol
rushing through my veins, making me feel all warm and
light-headed inside.

I forgot to check my phone, I missed the calls, and the
messages from Anthony.

Where are you? xx

Why aren't you answering
me? xx

You better not be talking to
boys!

For a moment the alcohol took me away, it made me forget that I hadn't snuggled up in bed with my boyfriend in more than a year, that I didn't know the next time I would be able to do that. I was now 18 years old, an adult, I could do what I wanted – well, everything except be with the man I loved.

I got drunk that night, so drunk that my head was spinning by the time we got to the nightclub, my feet unable to find the floor so easily any more.

'You're not coming in,' the bouncer said.

'But it's my birthday,' I slurred back.

But he shook his head. 'You're too drunk.'

I was back home and tucked up in bed before midnight on my eighteenth birthday. I rang Anthony and he couldn't stop laughing.

'You couldn't even get into a club on your eighteenth birthday!' he laughed. 'What a baby!'

And shame burned at my cheeks, not so much because of what had happened – maybe I was far too drunk to enjoy the club anyway – but because in his voice I knew he was happy that my night had been ruined: he didn't want me out celebrating my birthday, he didn't want me doing anything without him.

CHAPTER 3

JEALOUSY

I kept the phone glued to my hand from the minute I woke up that morning. Even in college, when it was tucked inside my black tunic, my hand was on it, waiting for the second when I felt that tiny vibration, when I looked down and saw it light up with a message from one person: Anthony. So I sat through lessons about the different layers of the skin, I waded through the epidermis, the dermis, the subcutaneous tissue, one hand making notes with my biro, curling the ink around the words, the other pinned to my phone. Because today was the day, after one long year, that Anthony was finally leaving prison.

I was sure of it this time, or 99 per cent sure. That's why I'd taken extra time to do my hair and make-up this morning, but even as my mascara wand had licked every eyelash I'd had to remind myself that there had been plenty of false starts before. Too many weeks when he'd told me that I wouldn't have to wait much longer, and yet those very same weeks had rolled round without his hand in mine, without the warmth of him by my side. But this week, today, even I had a good feeling about. And I was right.

The call came through at 11 o'clock when I was on my break. Anthony.

'It's today, Adele,' he said. 'Baby, they're letting me out!'

I felt my stomach twist and leap with excitement.

By the time I'd made my way to the admin office at college to feign illness and get signed off for the rest of the day, Anthony's Aunty Lorraine was waiting for me in her blue car by reception.

'You ready?' she said, when I sat down beside her and clicked my seat belt into place.

'I can't wait!' I said.

And I couldn't, not any longer, not when I'd already waited a year for Anthony. As we sped through the countryside and out onto the dual carriageway that led us towards Norwich Prison, I thought of everything we'd been through over the last 12 months, the good times and the bad. Not many couples make it through a whole year of being apart, especially not when they'd only been together a matter of weeks in the first place.

All the things that Anthony had written in his letters were right: what we had was special. I was 18 now, and yet for a year I'd saved myself for him. I hadn't been near another boy – how could I? *Why* would I? Not when I had him writing to me from prison, ringing me every night. Those phone calls, those letters, they were what I'd lived for, they were the fuel I needed to get through the tough times. Just one glance over the letter, just eating up some of the words that he'd written, was enough for me, it sated me, but it didn't have to be enough any more. Today, I was getting Anthony for real, in just moments his hand would be in mine and I wasn't going to let it go. Not this time. I smiled at that thought, and clutched my phone tighter, the only lifeline I'd had to him for months. What would I have done without it?

Finally, we drove down the long, straight road that led right up to the prison gates themselves. There they were, two huge brown doors, framed by the red brick of the imposing prison walls, and there, looking so small standing in front of them clutching a plastic bag, was Anthony.

The smile he had stretched across each cheek was wider than I'd ever seen before, and mirrored, I imagined, only by an identical one on my own face. He bounded over to us, reaching for the car door before we'd even properly stopped. But as he did so, I was already unclipping my seatbelt and leaping out of the door and into his arms. And then finally there he was, his body next to mine, squeezed into the tightest hug I'd ever known, one that told me he wasn't going to let go again either. As I felt his arms around me, finally, I couldn't stop the tears coursing down my cheeks.

'Oh baby!' he said, pulling a sad face and then kissing my cheeks. 'Come on, let's go home.'

He got into the back of the car beside me. After a year apart we weren't going to let the front seat of the car separate us. Instead we sat on the back seat together, holding hands, entwining our fingers, and squeezing every so often as we chatted to Lorraine in the front.

But it wasn't exactly home we were going to. Anthony had been released on condition that he stay at a bail hostel in Ipswich, 45 miles from my home in Lowestoft, but miles better than being locked up in a red-brick prison.

The bail hostel was down a short road next to a railway bridge. If it wasn't for the bars at the window it would look like a pretty ordinary house, but for the time being it was the only place that Anthony would be able to call home.

'It's just for a few months, baby,' he said, when he saw my face eyeing it from the outside. 'I'm going to prove I'm good and get out and then we'll get our own house together.'

I thought then of all the letters he'd sent me from prison, every single one I'd kept, stuffed inside a drawer in my bedroom at home, and buried within them were all our plans for the future; our dreams of a house, hot sunny holidays, and Anthony hadn't forgotten, that's what he wanted too. So for now I'd live with him in this hostel because he was right, it wouldn't be forever. He went inside to check in, then came out smiling.

'I don't have to be back until 9 pm,' he grinned.

So Lorraine put the car into gear and we were off back to Lowestoft. We headed to his dad's house, and there I stood back while Anthony gave everyone a hug, picking up his tiny baby sister and giving her a squeeze.

'It's good to be back,' he said, looking around, and his eyes falling on me.

'We've got some making up to do, ain't we, baby?'

I nodded and I must have blushed because Anthony reached out for my hand.

'Come on,' he said, indicating his bedroom upstairs. We left everyone else downstairs and up in his old room we had sex for the first time in a year. That was when he cried, when he came undone. While our bodies were still tangled together, I wrapped my arms around him, stroking his hair, wishing all the time that we could stay like this and that 9 pm wouldn't come around and steal him from me. And just as my mind drifted back to a time when we were free, when there was nothing and no one to keep us apart, he suddenly looked up at me. This time, his face was different, and when he spoke it wasn't in the same gentle way he had all day. It was cold, hard.

'You've blatantly had sex with someone else,' he said.

'What!'

'You have, you clearly have.'

'Anthony, what are you talking about? I haven't been with anyone, I've been waiting for you!'

He looked away.

'Anthony!' I tried, reaching for him, my fingertips brushing the tattoo dedicated to his mum, and my voice becoming instantly softer. 'Don't start this, you've been in prison and I've been waiting on you. You know I have ...'

When he turned around again, he was back to me, his face soft, his brow ironed out.

'Come on,' he smiled. 'I better be getting back to the hostel.'

I drove him back with Lorraine, stopping off at Asda to get him a cheap mobile phone.

'This way I can ring you all the time,' he said.

Even something as simple as walking around Asda, under the harsh supermarket lights, his hand in mine, having him back in my arms, felt amazing. I'd got my man back, everyone had been wrong and I had been right, I had waited and now I had him back. It was worth every single day without him.

We got him back to the hostel for 9 pm.

'I'll ring you when you get home,' he said, waving his new phone at me.

And he did, despite the fact that he was home, that he had other people to sit with or chat to in the hostel, it was still me he wanted. I went to sleep that night knowing that he was that step closer to me, that I could see him tomorrow, or the next day, or the next; that I could lie down with his arms wrapped around me, that there would be no prison guards standing over us, watching us. We were free, just a little bit more free, and soon we'd be even closer. I'd waited this long, and I just had to wait a little while longer.

We fell into a routine which mostly – due to the times Anthony needed to check into the hostel – meant I would travel over to Ipswich to see him. The journey took an hour and a half on the train, but it was always worth it. He'd usually keep me from getting bored by phoning me on the way there and on the way home, and he'd always be there to meet me from my train.

We had nowhere to go in the day as I wasn't allowed into the hostel, but we still had fun. We'd go swimming, or look round the shops. Sometimes Anthony would see a dress he liked for me.

'Do you like it?' he'd ask, holding it up. And when I said yes, he'd head straight over to the till and buy it for me.

There is romance to be found in wandering a city together with nowhere to go, the dinners or long lunches, sitting together in the darkness of a cinema holding hands, and in between walking round the shops planning what our life would be like when we could finally be together properly. On sunny days we'd get fish and chips and lie in the park together.

'Look at me being all romantic,' Anthony would laugh, and he really was, people didn't see the side of him that I did. They didn't know the soft side, they didn't know the letters he'd written to me from prison. But I did, I remembered every single stroke of his biro as each word had built a better picture of the life that we were working towards.

Mum never suspected that I was skipping college to go and meet Anthony, not when I left the house at 8 am in my black tunic and headed to the bus stop like I usually would; she didn't see me phoning the admin office to call in sick. On Tuesdays Anthony had to meet with his parole officer in Lowestoft and those days he didn't need to sign in, so we'd meet at his dad's and spend long afternoons in bed together before he had to go home.

But the demons were still there, the jealousy was only ever one wrong word away. Sometimes, just out of nowhere, when I'd spent an hour and a half on a train to visit him, he'd turn to me with dark eyes.

'The other day I got told you cheated on me when I was inside.'

'Anthony, I haven't, we've been through this!'

I'd perhaps roll my eyes at first, knowing we'd been here before. But that would just rile him more, so I'd plead and beg and try to convince him.

'I've waited for you all this time,' I'd say. 'Believe me I haven't done anything.'

'That's not what I heard.'

I'd start to cry, and then he'd just accuse me of being a baby.

'You feel guilty now, don't you,' he'd say. 'But you didn't feel guilty when I was inside, did you? Not when you were taking the piss out of me –'

'Anthony,' I'd sob. 'I haven't –'

'Don't lie to me!'

Round and round it went, any happy day ruined by him telling me that people had been talking about me to him. But I hadn't done anything. I didn't want to.

'I only ever wanted Anthony,' I cried once to his Aunty Claire.

She sighed and put her arms around me. 'He's just come out of prison, he's finding it hard to adjust.'

And on the good days, that's what he'd tell me too, he'd remind me that he had never felt like this about anyone.

'It's only because I love you so much that I worried you cheated on me,' he'd say.

'But I didn't,' I tried again. But I only ever got through to him until the next time.

Within weeks of his release it felt as if every day he had heard another rumour to present to me. Did he really hear them? Were people really saying these things? Or did he just enjoy watching me squirm? Even then I wasn't sure, so instead my mind searched for other reasons. What I did know was how vulnerable Anthony was, how much he needed me to stick by him when everyone else had deserted him. I knew he was afraid to love me, afraid to let go, so I just tried harder. Even when he'd row with me while I was on the train to see him in the mornings, if I said the wrong thing on the phone, or mentioned going out, or the wrong name from college, he'd fly off the handle at something.

'I'm not meeting you at the station,' he'd say, hanging up.

And on those days he wouldn't be there when the train turned up. So I had no choice but to walk to the bail hostel, to beg him to come out and see me, otherwise it would be a totally wasted day, and when he finally did I'd try extra hard to have a good time. And we would. I'd talk him round, I'd convince him that he had nothing to worry about, and then we'd walk past a man, and once they were a few steps away he'd turn to me:

'I saw the way you looked at him,' he'd say.

'What …!'

'Don't lie to me, I saw it,' he'd say.

Sometimes I'd get back on the train shattered from my day with him, but by the time I got home the phone calls would start, the romantic texts.

Love you baby, just finding
it hard getting out cos I
love you so much. xxx

And each and every time it made everything OK again. Until the next time.

Anthony wanted sex, but in Ipswich there was nowhere for us to go, but that never stopped him.

One day we were walking through the park in the town centre and we found a spot to lay down in the grass. Within minutes he was putting his hands all over me.

'Anthony!' I said, swiping them away. 'I'm not doing it here, I'm not like that!'

'What about me?' he said. 'I want sex.'

'But I'm not doing it outside in a park,' I said. 'Not where people can see us.'

'So I'll dump you,' he said. 'I'm free now, I can do what I want, if you don't give me sex I'll find someone else who wants to.'

He got up, and walked off, and before I knew it I was trailing after him, being persuaded into a bush or some muddy cut where stray branches offered little to protect my modesty.

Why did I do it? Because it was easier than dealing with his moods, or what he'd put me through for refusing him.

Once he'd had sex, while I pulled my jeans back up, feeling dirty, awful, he'd be all lovey dovey, walking out of the park with his arm around me, a big smile across his face, while I wanted to do anything to hide mine from the dog walkers who passed beside us, terrified in case they'd seen anything, or even that they'd guess from the look on my face.

I tried to say no to him. Once when I'd refused he turned away from me, and I went over to him and reached out to grab his arm.

'Why are you doing this, Anthony?' I said, and he pushed me. I don't think he meant to, it must have been a reflex, a reaction. But seconds later I was on the ground, watching his footsteps walking out of the park without a backwards glance. I headed back to the train station on my own, wondering how our day had gone so wrong, chastising myself for what I'd said or how I'd handled things. Was it so bad that he wanted to make love to me? Was it his fault we had nowhere to go?

He rang me on the train home, calling me names, telling me I was frigid.

'But you weren't when I was inside, were you? You were a right little slut then, I've heard just what a little slut you were.'

He'd hang up then, leaving me in tears.

But by the time the train pulled into Lowestoft, the long journey had reminded me of what his aunty said about how he was still adjusting to life on the outside. The train rumbling along the tracks had afforded me the chance to close my eyes and picture the tattoo with his mum's name. Nothing blotting the landscape but miles of flat countryside had made me remember just how much he'd suffered, and I'd told myself that things would change, when he trusted me, when he realised I wasn't going to leave him too. So when Anthony called that night as he always did, I'd tell him I understood, I heard myself saying sorry, and it was worth it, just to hang up and know everything was OK, that our life and our plans were still intact. That all I'd invested in over the last year was giving me some return. That I hadn't done the wrong thing by waiting for him. That after everything we'd gone through, we still had something that no one else did.

And in between those difficult times, there were the good days too, the times when he reminded me just how much I meant to him.

'You're the only one who has ever spent any time on me,' he'd say. 'You're the only person I've ever given my heart to. I loved my mum so much, but she left me, and that's why I'm angry sometimes because it feels like as soon as I get close to someone, they go.'

Those were the times when I wanted to reach down the phone line and bury him in my arms. I just had to make sure I didn't leave him like everyone else had.

'I only get angry because I'm so worried I'm going to lose you.'

'But can't you see that behaving like that is the way you will lose me, Anthony? I will go.'

But I never did.

And the next day it was always something else.

As the months rolled on, it did occur to me that I only ever saw Anthony on his terms. There were days when I didn't want to get the train over to Ipswich, to sit in a carriage as it rocked me back and forth, an hour and a half there, an hour and a half back. There were days when I wanted to see the friends who had been there for me when Anthony hadn't.

'I'm not coming over tomorrow,' I would tell Anthony. 'I've arranged to see my friends.'

'Tell your mates you're coming to see me,' he'd say.

And yet there were the times when I told him I was going to see him, and he'd tell me he was having his friends visit him.

'That's OK then, I'll get a lift with them, it'll be easier for me.'

'Nah Adele, I want to see my mates tomorrow.'

That was it, no arguing.

Back in the outside world, Anthony was on Facebook, and constantly questioning me about people I was friends with. One day one of my old school friends – a guy – commented on my page.

'You're using it to speak to boys,' Anthony said.

'What? I'm not, I don't even speak to that guy any more. He was someone from school ...'

But Anthony was adamant, always in the back of his mind there was someone else. If I didn't want sex it was because I'd been having it with someone else, but who? When?

'You need to delete your Facebook account,' he said, finally.

'Why?'

'Because you don't need it like I do, you can see or speak to your friends, I can't.'

I told myself it didn't matter, that I didn't need Facebook. I didn't have anything to hide, and if I made a fuss I knew it would look like I did.

'OK,' I said. 'I'll delete it, but you've got to delete yours too.'

He shook his head. 'If you want our relationship to work, if you really love me as much as you say you do, then you'll delete it.'

So I did, because I did love him. I just had to get Anthony to see that.

It did work for a while, doing what Anthony said. It did make him trust me; it did seem to make him calmer. The harder I worked, the better things were, or at least for a while.

One Tuesday morning when I was at college, Anthony texted. He was in Lowestoft for the day because he had to meet with his parole officer.

I've got you a present. It's
black. xx

What is it? xx

I'm not telling you, but I
love it, you're gonna love it.

xx

At break time me and the girls tried to figure out what it could be.

'If it's black it has to be underwear,' Nicole said.

'Yeah, especially if he said he loves it and you're gonna love it,' said Amie.

'Yeah, it must be underwear,' I nodded.

When I came out of college, there he was, waiting by the main doors, just like he'd done more than a year ago, before prison, before it had all gone so wrong. Except he wasn't holding any bags or anything.

'Where's my present?' I asked.

He grinned. 'You're going to love it,' he said, and with that he peeled back his T-shirt and pulled at the waistband of his jeans. There it was, just above his boxer shorts. It took a moment to sink in, to recognise the letters of my own name, but there they were, inked on him in thick black letters, 'Adele', with a love heart next to them.

'Well, what do you think?' Anthony asked, running his fingers along each letter. The skin was pink and sore, covered in a gel and clingfilm.

'Oh my God,' I said. 'What the hell?'

'Do you like it?' he said. 'I love you, you waited on me, and we're going to be together forever ...'

But for some reason I wasn't flattered, instead I just felt sick, a creeping sense of bile welling inside my stomach, threatening to make its way up to my throat. Anthony was still looking at me expectantly, and I didn't know what to say, because this had come with a price tag, I knew it. This wasn't just a gesture he'd made for me, it came with a catch.

'You'll have to get one too now,' he said. 'With my name on it.'

There it was, the catch. The real reason that he'd had it done, so that he could brand my own skin with his name.

'Oh Anthony, I don't know, I –'

'What do you mean? I've done this for you, of course you're going to get one for me!'

He was determined I should get one too. Whenever I saw him, he started again. Sometimes he'd just hassle me about when I was getting it done.

'What time do you finish college on Tuesday? I'll book you into a tattoo parlour for afterwards.'

Other times, he found places for me to have it done near his bail hostel in Ipswich.

'You can get it done next week when you visit. I'll book it for you.'

And then there were the times when he was just so annoyed with me that I hadn't done it yet that he'd start an argument.

'You don't love me, do you? You can't prove to me that there's no one else?'

'What? Anthony, no! It's not that, it's my mum, she'll go mad.'

'Do you care what she thinks more than me?'

'But I'm scared it'll hurt,' I tried.

'I went through that pain for you, can't you do the same for me?'

On and on it went. In the end I agreed to get it done just to shut him up.

'I'll get a tiny one, on my bum,' I said.

'No! You need to get it where people can see it!'

It didn't help that my friends thought what he'd done was really romantic.

'Awww, he had your name tattooed on him, that's so sweet …'

'My boyfriend wouldn't do that for me …'

And when they said that, it did make me feel like it was actually quite flattering, that I was special. I just wished he didn't have to keep pestering me to have one done too. It wasn't like I asked him to go and get a tattoo, and there must have been something, very deep in the back of my mind, that told me that I didn't want his name permanently inked on my skin. And perhaps, somehow, he knew it.

But in between times, when he wasn't nagging me, we were happy. The months rumbled on in the bail hostel; there were only two or three months left of staying in there now, not much longer until we'd get our own place. I carried on with my beauty course, hanging out with friends who were dating boys their own age, not a 20-year-old guy, not someone who talked about getting a house and filling it with all our things, or got their name tattooed on them. I'd waited patiently for my man, I was still waiting, and when we had our own house, once we were living together and Anthony knew I was in bed next to him each night, then he wouldn't need to worry. I just needed to hang on a little while longer.

A couple of weeks later I was in my college class when my phone started ringing. Anthony. What was wrong? It was a Tuesday, he knew I was in class. I didn't answer. But then the texts started.

Adele, you slut.

What?

I made my excuses to leave the class and went outside to call him.

'Anthony, what the –'

'You slept with my brother, you dirty slut!'

'What?!'

'Don't lie to me!'

'I'm not … where are you?'

'I'm in the pub.'

'Anthony, what are you doing, you know you're going to get tested later, you're not allowed to drink –'

'You're a slut, Adele, a dirty slut. I can't believe you slept with my brother.'

'Anthony, I didn't. What are you talking about? Where are you? Which pub are you in?'

He told me before hanging up. I went and signed out sick from college and headed there to meet him. He came outside to speak to me, bringing with him a cloud of whisky. His eyes were glazed, green with anger, they weren't the same eyes I knew, the ones he looked at me with when we were curled up in bed together, they were dangerous, frightening.

'What have you done?' he spat at me, pushing me hard in the chest. 'You slept with my brother. You slept with John.'

'Anthony, I didn't, I hardly know him, look …'

I pulled me phone out of the bag so I could show him the messages on Facebook. I'd only met John a couple of months before while Anthony was inside; he'd come up to me outside a takeaway and introduced himself. He made friends with me on Facebook and I'd accepted and we'd exchanged two messages where he'd asked about Anthony and I'd said it was nice to meet him. That was it. I had to show Anthony. I wouldn't sleep with his brother.

But as I went to show him the phone – my brand new iPhone – he pulled it out of my hand and hurled it into the road, smashing it to pieces. He was crazed, furious, and I was scared. And then suddenly a taxi was passing with his mates inside and he just jumped into it.

'Where are you going?' I screamed after him.

But he was gone, and I stood in the middle of the road, my smashed phone at my feet, tears running down my cheeks because it felt so unfair, I hadn't slept with his brother, I hadn't done anything but be faithful to Anthony. Why did he make me suffer? Why didn't he ever believe me? And yet even though he'd just accused me of that, even though he'd just pushed me like I meant nothing to him, even though he'd smashed my new phone, I was worried about him getting in trouble for breaking his bail conditions, for drinking, for being so out of control. What was he going to do?

My answer came the next day. I'd put my sim card into my old phone, and a few hours later Anthony called.

'I'm going to prison now because of you and your slutty ways,' he said. 'The police are looking for me.'

'Anthony, what have you done?'

What he'd done was left me that day and gone to his dad's house. There he'd beaten up his brother. For no reason other than he'd messaged me, because what Anthony had heard was nothing but rumours.

He rang me again later that day after the police had caught him.

'I'm only allowed one phone call,' he said. 'I love you. I'm really sorry, my head weren't right, I'd been hearing rumours about you and John, people trying to butt into our relationship ... I'm sorry.'

He broke down because this meant he was going back to prison, and for some reason, on the other end of the phone it was suddenly me feeling guilty. I shouldn't have messaged his brother on Facebook, if only I hadn't spoken to him outside of the takeaway.

'It's not your fault, babe,' he said, before hanging up as if he could read my thoughts. 'It's John's.'

CHAPTER 4

ISOLATION

I cried for a week when Anthony went back to prison. I couldn't eat, I couldn't sleep.

'This has got to be it now, Adele,' Mum said. 'Surely you can see this is him now? He's not going to change.'

'But he wants to, Mum.'

'You can't wait for him again.'

She sighed and busied herself in the kitchen.

But she also knew she couldn't stop me. She saw the way I dashed for the house phone when he called from prison, how I ran upstairs and locked myself in my room whenever he called my mobile. She didn't know of course that our conversations were usually spent arguing, with him telling me not to go out or to get a tattoo with his name. But in among those arguments that every couple has, we laughed together, I teased him, he called me cheeky. We loved each other.

Up in my bedroom I looked through the letters he'd sent me, the ones where he'd opened up and told me about his life before he met me. No one had ever believed in Anthony before I came along. I remember how he'd told me how his dad had made him harden up by fighting with his brother as a kid. The kind of life he came from was a million miles away from how I'd been brought up. I knew that's why he always teased me and said I was posh or stuck up, but didn't Anthony deserve to have something good in his life too? Didn't he deserve to have me there for him? And hadn't I promised him I would be?

Yet at the same time, I knew why people would think I was stupid for not leaving him now. I'd waited 14 months for him to come out of prison before, I'd waited all that time for someone I'd only been with a few weeks, and now, just two months later, he was back in prison. But I could see the good in him where other people couldn't.

I did love Anthony, but there was also that stubborn part of me that had already invested so much that I didn't want to give up now. I couldn't. I couldn't bear for people to say I told you so, and I knew they were all dying to. I suddenly resented my friends and their perfect boyfriends. Why couldn't my boyfriend be normal like theirs? Why did mine have to keep screwing everything up? I was jealous of the life they had with their boyfriends.

'Come on, we've got our holiday to look forward to,' Remi said.

We'd booked a week in Faliraki. I'd been nervous about telling Anthony I was going away, and I guess in some ways him being in prison made it easier for me to go. He didn't have a mobile now he was back inside, so he could only call from the prison phone, but whenever he did he'd always get into my head.

'Promise me you won't go out when you go to Faliraki, Adele, promise on my mum's grave. Say it.'

'OK, I promise.'

'I love you,' he said. 'I just don't want you getting drunk and talking to boys and making a stupid mistake.'

'Anthony. I won't. You say you love me but you don't trust me.'

'I just know what you're like when you're drunk. So just say you won't go out, say you won't get drunk. If you don't go out then I don't need to worry, do I?'

'OK,' I agreed. 'I promise on your mum's grave I won't go out.'

'And you'll get a tattoo when you're back,' he added.

Faliraki was my first girls' holiday abroad. It should have been an amazing week. I went with Remi, Amie and Jessie, three of my best friends. We'd been looking forward to it for months, a chance to relax and lie in the sun after all our hard work at college, meals out as the sun dipped behind the clouds. Jessie had a boyfriend, so like me she didn't want to go out meeting boys, but the other two did – they were determined to go out every night.

But then, two days before we left for Greece, Anthony rang me from a mobile number.

'I've got myself a phone!' he said. 'I can call you whenever I want now.'

He was delighted, but something inside me, some part that had been looking forward to my holiday, just evaporated into thin air. I knew that as long as Anthony had a mobile phone he wouldn't let me enjoy my week away.

And he didn't. Even if I was in the pool and he rang and I didn't answer he'd be hassling me.

'Why didn't you answer? Were you talking to boys?'

'Anthony,' I said. 'I was swimming in the pool, I'd left my phone beside my sun lounger.'

But he never believed me.

Jessie was texting her boyfriend too, but he wasn't ringing her constantly like Anthony was me. Each night we would get dressed up and go out for dinner, but I had to promise Anthony I'd be home by midnight.

'Come on, stay out,' Remi would plead as Jessie and I went back after our meal. 'The night is only just getting started.'

But just like Cinderella, I knew I had to be back at our hotel by the time the clock struck 12, in time for Anthony to ring and check on me. Even if I answered the phone on the main drag of clubs on my walk back to the apartment he wasn't happy, not when he could hear people partying in the background, even if I promised him faithfully that I was on my way home.

'Who are you with? Are you talking to boys? Have you been drinking? You promised me you wouldn't go out. How do you think it makes me feel when I'm in here and you're out with boys?'

'Anthony, I'm not –'

But he'd go on and on until he wore me down, and so the next night I'd make sure I was home well before midnight because it was too exhausting to defend myself, to convince him that I hadn't done anything wrong. At least if I was back in our apartment, if he could hear nothing but the safety of silence around me, he would be happy, there would be nothing to have a go at me about. I wouldn't have had any reason to annoy him or make him stressed, and then we'd have a nice chat. It wouldn't last long because he was calling Greece but at least he'd be in a good mood.

Except that on the last night when he called I wasn't at the apartment. I'm not sure if it was before midnight that he called, or if I just hadn't heard my phone ringing in my bag, but I missed his call and he went mad.

'You said you'd be back at midnight!' he stormed when he finally got hold of me.

'I was, I just missed your –'

'Don't lie to me, Adele. You promised you'd be back at 12! You were sleeping with someone, weren't you? You've been sleeping with someone all week.'

'No, Anthony! How could I when I've been speaking to you on the phone all week? I wouldn't, I –'

'I can't trust you, Adele. You lie to me, you promise you'll be back at 12 and then you're not! You're a slut. I can't trust you. I don't want to be with you any more. We've over.' And with that he hung up.

The last night of my holiday, after doing everything he asked of me all week, he'd dumped me.

'There's a few hours left. Don't sit in moping, come out with us,' Remi and Amie tried to persuade me.

'I don't feel like it,' I sighed.

I didn't. Anthony knew how to make me feel bad. He knew what to say, how to blame me, how to make me feel like everything was my fault. And maybe it was? Maybe I could have been better, maybe I should have made sure the phone was in my hand so I wouldn't have missed his call because if I had, he wouldn't have dumped me. If I had, he wouldn't have put the phone down on me, he wouldn't have blamed me, he wouldn't have called me a slut or said everything was my fault. If I had, we would still be together.

'You can do better than him, Adele,' Remi said.

And I think, deep down inside, I knew it. I always knew it. But there was something stopping me too. Fear.

'You don't know what he's capable of,' I told the girls.

They didn't say any more because they knew Anthony was dangerous, they saw how people feared him in our town, they knew I was right. So it was easier just to be with Anthony, to hang on for the good times, to remember what we had right at the beginning and to tell myself that it would be like that again one day if I just waited a little bit more, if I just did what he said. I was frightened to be with him, but I was frightened not to be with him too. There was a little part of me, right deep down, that liked having a boyfriend, that wanted to be like all the rest of my friends, that wondered what life would be like without this attention, without the drama, without someone writing me letters from prison or ringing me every day. I saw the boys my friends went out with who weren't bothered about them, who never called. Look at the man I had, he never left me alone, surely that meant that he really *really* loved me? Didn't it? He wouldn't be so possessive if he didn't care so much.

And anyway, it was OK when my friends said forget about him, but how would I ever go out with anyone after Anthony? He'd tell me if I even spoke to another guy that he'd beat him up and I knew he meant it. He was in prison for beating his own brother up after all. It was easier to stick with Anthony, to invest some more, to try and please him, than even attempt to leave him.

During the good times we'd make all our plans, we'd talk about the place we were going to get together; two bedrooms so Scotty could stay over and Anthony could have weights in the spare room. We'd fantasise about our wedding and getting married in Rome. I'd tell Anthony that I wanted to travel and he'd tell me that we could go anywhere except for America because he'd never get a visa due to his convictions. We'd say we'd have two kids, one of each, and Anthony would call them little Rileys.

And I'd live for those good times, when Anthony would tell me I was the most beautiful girl in the world. But it was never for long, because the bad times were only ever a phone call or a letter away. We'd argue on the phone and he'd rant and rave at me and I'd shudder while I listened to him smashing up his cell in a rage because I hadn't answered the phone when he called, or one of his mates had told him they'd seen me out speaking to another boy, even if it was just one of my friends' boyfriends, or I'd said the wrong thing. It was easier just to do what he told me to.

When we flew home from Faliraki, the girls said it was their best holiday ever; for me, it was the worst. I knew who to blame, and yet, even though he'd dumped me, I felt I had to let him know I was home. Two days later, I sat round the dining table with Mum and Dad having dinner. Suddenly we heard a crash in the front of the house, the sound of breaking glass. The whole house seemed to shake.

'What the …?' Dad said, dashing towards the front door.

Me and Mum raced after him, and there in the hallway shards of glass lay scattered across the floor, a huge empty space where once the glass panel in the front door had been, and at the foot of it all an orange brick on the carpet.

Dad was already out the house and up the street. He caught the girl who did it and called the police; she just said she'd been paid to do it, she wouldn't say by who. But a phone call a few hours later gave us a few more clues. Mum picked it up.

'This is because Adele went on holiday,' a stranger's voice said before hanging up.

Anthony was behind it. This changed everything, it marked the start of something else. He'd brought this to my family home. My parents were fuming.

'You can't have any more to do with him, Adele!' Dad said. 'He's crazy!'

But I didn't answer because I was scared, because it was no longer just about me: I'd seen what Anthony would do, the people who he would hurt if I upset him. I had to protect my family, and if the only way I did that was to stay with him and keep him happy then I would. No one knew what he was capable of. Today it had been a brick through the window. What would he do tomorrow if I didn't do what he said? Who would he hurt then? In all honesty, I felt trapped, but what could I do? He'd done this because I went on holiday. What would he do if I ended our relationship for good?

He called a few days later, crying, telling me he loved me after all.

'I am just so scared of losing you that it makes me get angry, but you're the only person who has had my heart and I'm scared of losing that.'

'But Anthony, you got someone to put a brick through my parents' window.'

'I just got angry because I was scared of losing you. I'm in here, in these four walls, and my girlfriend had gone to a party island. I just lash out, Adele. I'm doing anger management courses here, I'm trying to get help in prison. I know I need help.'

I sighed. It was done now, I was back from my holiday, the mess was cleared up off the carpet, and Anthony had explained why he'd done it. We had to move on, the holiday was over. There was nothing to worry about now, I wasn't going on holiday again so he didn't need to get scared or angry. I just had to do everything right, and then we'd all be OK. There would be no more bricks through the window, Anthony wouldn't be in there forever, things would get back to normal.

'OK,' I said. 'Let's try again.'

But even as I hung up the phone I knew somewhere deep inside that all he'd done was to scare me into staying with him.

I hated visiting Anthony in prison, it made me feel disgusting. I hated the way that they shunted us into pens while they shut one prison gate and opened another. I hated how we were given numbers rather than names. I hated looking around at the people I rubbed shoulders with. I hated the fact that all the prisoners looked the same in their fluorescent bibs. I hated the way they frisked you before they let you in. I hated the way the prison officers looked at you like you were the scum of the earth. But I mostly hated it because, during my visits to Anthony, that's exactly how I felt. I felt embarrassed to be there.

But today when I walked into the waiting room there was none of that. The female prison officer, who was usually really moody, was much friendlier than ever before.

'Anthony's really looking forward to seeing you today,' she grinned. 'He keeps talking about you.'

'Oh right,' I said, unsure why she was being so nice.

Even when I walked in and sat at the table, things felt different. Anthony arrived and he looked really happy. We had a good visit and unusually there were no arguments: he wasn't pestering me to get a tattoo or questioning me whether I'd been out or spoken to anyone. It was like old times, except of course that he couldn't just get up and walk out with me.

But then, suddenly, he did get up and I noticed that a dozen faces around the room looked up as he did. Then I realised that the other convicts and their visitors had all turned around to look at us like they knew something was about to happen, something out of the ordinary. I looked over my shoulder at the prison guards standing by the walls, but they didn't tell him to sit down like they usually would. Instead, they smiled and nodded at him, and I wondered again why everything felt so strange today, so different. And then, when I looked back round at Anthony, I saw for myself; he was down on one knee, looking up at me with a beaming smile, a rose that he'd made out of matchsticks in his hands, reaching up to me.

'Adele Bellis,' he said. 'Will you be my wife?'

I can't remember saying anything. I don't think that I answered. Instead, I felt like I was drowning. I knew there was an answer welling deep inside, and I knew it wasn't the one he was waiting for, so fear, confusion, shock stopped it from leaping out. But that didn't seem to matter anyway, because I looked up, my head swimming, and all I could see was the female prison officer marching over to me smiling from ear to ear.

'Congratulations!' she said.

And with that all the convicts and their friends and family were up on their feet, clapping and cheering. I turned back to Anthony who was looking round at his friends, punching the air, and I realised in that second I hadn't even answered him. Everyone had presumed I'd said yes, but inside I was screaming anything but, I was screaming no.

I mumbled something then. But nobody seemed to hear me. I was drowning in their cheers and congratulations.

'We'll see when you get out,' I tried.

But Anthony was wrapping me in a hug and the last of the applause was dying down, and people had gone back to chatting with their visitors, a lighter, happier feeling in the room. I turned to Anthony and he was grinning, and all I kept thinking was how embarrassing it was, how I'd never imagined I'd be proposed to like this, in here, and how there was no way I was marrying a convict. I knew then, in that instant, that Anthony was not the man I was going to marry. But it was like everyone else had decided I was, the decision had been made, the deal was done and I was too scared to undo it all.

I'd only wanted to help Anthony, I could see that there was a nice person inside there; even then, across that prison visiting table, I saw again the good side of him. He wasn't the thug that everyone thought, he wasn't really that angry person, I knew he could be good too. But good enough to marry? Nothing had been further from my mind.

When the visit was over a few minutes later, I shuffled out, feeling congratulations from strangers patting me on my shoulder. I was still lost for words, still horrified by a prison proposal, yet too dumbfounded to tell him – or anyone – I hadn't said yes.

I didn't tell anyone when I got home. I just figured, as long as Anthony was happy, he wasn't having a go at me. The rest would sort itself out in time. Or at least I hoped it would.

I need to ask you some questions, Adele ...

Are you going to stop going out to pubs and clubs until I get out no matter what reason you or your mates have for going there?

Are you going to stay off facebook?

Will you stop talking to boy's mates or your mate's boyfriend whoever they are?

Will you get my name tattooed before you come on the next visit?

Before you say yes think about what you really want, if you can do that and stop all the rumours before I get out nothing can stop us from being happy ...

A few days later ...

Everything I have asked you to do since I came back in you done the opposite, some of it may seem small or stupid, but I done well, tried to do it so we could be happy when I got out. You say I'm the one you wanna be with so why not prove it? Why you so determined to wreck what we have built …? I'm back in here because of what I came out to before … I'm not saying it's your fault I'm back in here Adele, but if you didn't play stupid games like you are now I would still be out there now. Ok, I fucked up but can you honestly blame me? I thought I was coming out to the perfect girl and I did then all the shit happened, my world broke into bits and before I knew it I was locked up with a broken heart, everything I thought I had and knew was gone.

Another …

I'm just fed up of ringing my mates and them telling me shit Adele, so please sort your shit out if you really wanna be with me then stay off Facebook for good, stop talking to boys while I'm in here. I don't care who they are, what you were talking about or whose boyfriend they are, no excuses this time just stay away from them. You have to think about where I am and what I'm told and how that makes me feel and look. If you're serious about it then do this if not just say and I'll leave you alone. You can't have it both ways cos soon as I hear anything I swear I'm gone.

Another …

Hi baby, well I spoke to you this morning, you were going into town to book in for this tattoo. I really hope you've done it to prove to me there ain't no one else, or ever gonna be. I love you so, so, so much Adele, you are my

world, but if you don't book in for this tattoo today, I will
know you are seeing someone else, and I will be gone. You
keep saying wait but if there ain't no one else what are you
waiting for? Anyway, hopefully you did and everything will
be ok but if not, I'm a fucking mug.

On and on and on he went: if I just stopped going out with
my friends then everything would be OK; if I just stopped
talking to other boys – even if they were my friends'
boyfriends – everything would be OK; if I just got a tattoo …
But however much I tried to change, to abide by what
Anthony was asking of me for an easy life, something deep
down must have told me not to get his name engraved in ink
on my skin.

Instead I had to learn how to get what I wanted. He hated
me seeing my friends. If he ever called me and I was at Remi's,
having a takeaway, just a night in together, he'd pester me.

'I thought you were talking to me tonight?'

'OK, I'll be home by 9 pm,' I'd tell him finally.

But if I wasn't there, if Mum had agreed to come and pick
me up but had stopped at the shops on the way to get me and
I wasn't home in my bedroom by 9 pm when he called, then
Anthony would be fuming.

'You lied to me, Adele! That's why I can't trust you! You
said you'd be back by nine but you lied!'

On and on and on it went. Was it any wonder that it just
became easier not to go out in the first place?

But then there were the special occasions, like my best
friends' eighteenth birthdays.

'You have to be there,' they'd beg me, and I'd agree.

So when Anthony was ranting at me, I'd take it, I'd say sorry, I'd tell him I'd got the tattoo, I'd say anything just so that he would give me permission to have a night out with my friends. And if I did all those things, he would. Me and the girls would get excited, we'd plan how we were going to get ready together like the old days, which pubs and clubs we'd go to, what we'd wear. But even on the night Anthony would change his mind.

'You said I could go.'

'No, I didn't.'

He'd lie, or start a row for no reason, and he knew that by the time I hung up the phone I wouldn't be able to go out, I'd be too worried about the hassle I'd get from him, the fact that he'd be ringing my phone constantly, and then starting a row if I didn't answer, or the fact that anywhere I went he'd get his friends to watch me, various pairs of eyes watching my every move and reporting back to Anthony in prison.

He didn't even want me going out with my mum and dad. When it came to the World Cup we were all going down to the pub to watch it together; everyone was dressing up, England were playing, the place would be a sea of white and red St George flags, but just as we were about to leave the house my mobile started ringing. I ignored it, knowing it would be Anthony saying I couldn't go. But then the house phone started ringing too. Mum and Dad sighed; they knew it was him as no one else called the house. I quickly grabbed it before they got angry with me.

'You better not be going out.'

'I'm going to watch the football, I told you I was going.'

'If you go out then that's it between us.'

'Anthony, I'm going out with my parents –'

And then the phone would go dead, he'd make me suffer for disobeying him. But how could I not go when Mum and Dad were standing at the door ready?

There were plenty of times when I didn't go, though, when I'd be excited about a night out and then tell my friends I had a headache at the last minute, when I'd take off my make-up and sit in my bedroom, and Anthony wouldn't even call that night because I'd already annoyed him by wanting to go out in the first place.

No matter what I said about you going to Amie's that night, I still think it was wrong. But you'll still have a place in my heart, maybe not the same, cos I think your mates are too important to you. Maybe one day when you're properly ready for a relationship, you will choose your boyfriend over your friends. Take care, stay strong, don't be lead astray by them, you're worth more than that.

But of course the next day he'd be pestering me to get back together with him, and I did.

CHAPTER 5

CRITICISM

I looked out of the window of my Lowestoft College class-room, closed my eyes and allowed myself for a moment just to dream. It all sounded so perfect, days with nothing to stare out at but a deep blue sea and the sky above; others spent docking into the ports of pretty colourful harbours; days off spent exploring beaches, and nights spent sailing through thick black nights broken only by the stars. It sounded so ... so free.

'The money's not bad either,' Nicole leaned over and whispered to me, her voice and the rain slashing at the window quickly snapping me out of the fantasy.

'Yeah, but wouldn't it just be nice to get away from all this?'

A recruitment officer from a cruise liner company had come to do a presentation to our class. They were searching beauty colleges for new therapists on board their ships, a chance to put into practice all that we'd learnt over the last three years in our first proper jobs.

I closed my eyes and pictured it again, a life away from here, away from everything, everyone.

'Why don't you apply then?' Laura said, as if reading my thoughts.

'How can I?' I said.

She looked at me puzzled for a second before her brows unfurrowed themselves. I didn't need to say any more, she knew what, or rather who, I was referring to. I didn't need to remind her that I wasn't free, that this wasn't a life I could choose, unlike so many of my classmates who were turning the recruitment leaflets over in their hands and whispering excitedly among one another. And *pfft*, just like that, my dream disappeared, the chance to travel the world, to earn money doing what I loved, to be in the sunshine, to meet new people. No, my life was here, waiting for Anthony. He wouldn't agree to my having a night out with my friends, so there was no chance he'd let me go away and work on a cruise ship. That's all it was, a dream.

Over the last few weeks he'd kept telling me that he was due for release, but this time I knew better than to believe him. Anyway, despite the fact that I'd been waiting all this time for him – now, give or take a few months, coming up to almost two and a half years – deep down I wasn't actually sure what was better, him being in prison telling me what to do, or outside doing the same. I knew this time what he would be like; the moods, the demands for sex, the accusations that I'd been cheating on him the whole time he was away, or just occasionally, that good time, the nice meal out or a flash of the man I'd fallen for. But even I could admit that's all it was these days, a flash, a moment, not anything to hold onto. And yet it was enough to keep me waiting for him, that of course and the fear of what he'd do if I didn't, and it was increasingly difficult to separate the two these days, the love and the fear.

Sometimes, in clearer moments, I knew I was taking the easy option and I hated myself for it. I hated hearing myself apologise for something I hadn't done just to keep the peace when he called, or sweetening him up just to be granted permission to go out with my friends. But those conversations, those compromises, had become such a normal part of my life now.

And it wasn't like there weren't any good times. There were still the letters from prison, the love that was poured into them. If he wasn't calling me every night, then who else would? At least *he* wanted to speak to me for hours every night, at least *he* loved me and told me I was beautiful, that I was special, that I was the only woman he'd ever loved. But then, I had to ask myself, why did it always feel like such an impossible task to please him? Why was nothing ever good enough? Why was I constantly telling myself to try harder?

But I would. I'd keep on trying, because I knew the good side of Anthony, and I wanted everything we'd been planning. I knew that this time when he got out of prison things would be different, that he *wanted* them to be different, that he'd already told me he wasn't going to hang around with his old mates who let him lose hours to drink or told him lies about me. This time there would be holidays and getting our own place, everything we'd spent the last two years talking about. He'd change now, I knew it. I'd waited for him, he had to.

So given all that, it was hard to explain two weeks later, when I got a call on my mobile out of the blue, why my stomach didn't flip in excitement. We'd been arguing a lot in the days beforehand, so we hadn't been speaking every day as usual, and then I answered my phone.

'I'm out, baby! They let me out this morning!'

Instead, my stomach twisted in fear.

'I'm at Dad's, come round now … I'm out, baby! You've got your man back!'

I tried to sound pleased, and a part of me was, but a bigger part of me was worried and as I walked slowly round to his dad's I knew why – it was because a few weeks ago my friends had persuaded me to book a holiday to Ibiza, and I hadn't yet told Anthony. I'd thought with him in prison it would just be like before when I went to Faliraki, that he'd be calling me each night, but at least I'd be there. But if he was out there's no way he'd let me go.

He met me at the top of his dad's road, a huge smile on his face that just instantly alleviated any of my fears and reminded me of the man I loved, the good Anthony.

'I'm out, baby!' he said, scooping me up into his arms and hugging me so tight that I just knew this time he wasn't going to let go. 'I love you, Adele, I've missed you so much.'

I melted into his body. 'Oh Anthony, I've missed you so much too.'

We walked back to his dad's, our arms wrapped around each other so tight as if nothing could pull us apart this time. It felt different, better, after everything we'd been through, we'd survived. That had to mean something, right?

But then at the back of my mind there was the holiday in Ibiza. How could I have ruined everything by booking it? Or at least that's how it felt now. Anthony was in such a good mood those first few days, we were so happy, I didn't want anything to ruin it – I was *determined* not to ruin it – so I didn't tell him.

And it was wonderful: I did have my man back, I had the happy Anthony, the good guy, the one who preferred to lay tangled up in bed with me in a hotel room where we had some privacy, who didn't leap out of bed when his mates called but snuggled further under the duvet with me, and I told myself I'd been right to wait, that it was worth it.

But then, a few days after he got out, he did meet up with his mates. He'd been away a long time and it wasn't like he didn't deserve to see them.

'Just remember, Anthony,' I said. 'No drinking, you promised.'

'Don't worry, Cheeky,' he said, dropping a kiss on my nose.

But a few hours later the phone calls started.

'My mates have been telling me what's been going on while I was in prison,' he slurred. Drunk, again.

'Anthony, you said you wouldn't drink …'

'Don't give me that, Adele!' he snapped. 'Who are these boys you've been talking to? Have you been fucking someone behind my back? I know you've been making a mug of me.'

'Anthony, I haven't, you know I haven't. Where are you? Come home.'

'Come home? To you? To a slut? No thanks.'

And then the phone went dead.

Not that he was finished with me. Over and over it went, phone calls, texts. When we saw each other it was more of the same. On and on he'd go at me, accusations, flashes of anger in his eyes, the same wild look that I feared, that made me stammer and shake and willing to say anything so things could go back to how they were a few days before.

And then, everything went quiet.

He went out with his mates one night, and I didn't hear from him the next morning. I assumed he'd drunk too much, that he was hungover.

The next phone call I got was from him in prison.

'Adele, I'm back inside. I'm so sorry.'

He'd broken his bail conditions. I didn't know what he'd done, I didn't care because this was it now.

'After everything we've been through? You've only been out a week!'

'I know, I'm sorry, but if you just wait –'

'No, Anthony,' I said. 'That's it now. I've waited long enough!'

And I absolutely meant it.

I was 19 years old and I'd spent nearly two and a half years waiting for my boyfriend to get out of prison. Two and a half years while my friends got on with their lives, while they had nights out, holidays, different jobs, boyfriends, and enough was enough.

Three weeks later I went on holiday to Ibiza with five of my best friends, and we had a dream holiday. There was no going back to the apartment by midnight; there was no apologising for not answering my phone. If I stayed out late or chatted to guys around the pool I didn't need to feel worried. And I did, I did chat to lots of guys, and it felt nice not to have someone watching me on Anthony's behalf, not reporting back to him.

There were a group of Geordie lads that we became friends with on the holiday, and I got close to one of them. We slept together much of that week – the first man I'd been with since Anthony and I had become a couple – and it felt good, really good. I felt like a 19-year-old girl, I felt normal, I felt free. I didn't have to keep my phone with me at all times, in fact most of the time I left it in the hotel.

There were just two phone calls all week, and they were both from Anthony's sister, Michelle, but I told her I was on holiday, I didn't have time to talk. I didn't want to either, I didn't want anything to remind me of Anthony during this holiday because I felt so angry at him. But more than that, I felt stupid for waiting for him, stupid for believing him. My mum had been right all along: this was just what Anthony was like, I was never ever going to change him.

I arrived home after ten days, tanned, happy, strong, and ready for my next adventure. Yet the past wasn't willing to stay there. I'd only been back a few days and my mobile started ringing.

'I just want to know if you had a good holiday, Adele.'

'Anthony, we're over, what are you ringing me for?'

I hung up, but then his sister, Michelle, started ringing me.

'I know you've broken up,' she said. 'But I've got loads of letters here from Anthony ...'

'I'm sorry, Michelle, but I don't want them. I'm not with Anthony any more, I don't want anything to do with Anthony.'

But she wouldn't leave it there. A few days later she called again.

'Please, Adele,' she said. 'He just wants you to read them. You don't have to reply, just read them. Please.'

I sighed, then agreed to go and get them from her house if nothing else but to make her stop calling me. Jessie agreed to give me a lift.

'I'll wait outside,' she said when we pulled up.

I'd only met Michelle a handful of times before, she hadn't long moved down from Scotland and this was her new house. She was also seven months pregnant and peered out of the door at me over her massive bump.

'Adele! Hi, oh thanks for coming! Come in and see my new place!'

I glanced back at Jessie, before stepping into her house. The door closed behind me. Inside she gave me a guided tour through the living room, into the dining room, and finally to the back of the house where the kitchen was. There she handed me the letters, but as I took them I felt a whack to my stomach and realised she'd kneed me. I was suddenly bent double, completely blindsided, the breath taken out of me, I fell to the ground. And then it started: a full-blown assault on me as I lay writhing on the floor, kicks and punches, her shoe in my face, my stomach.

'What are you doing?' I managed in between the shock and the punches.

'You fucked my brother over,' she spat. 'And if you fuck him over, I'll fuck you over.'

The punches and kicks continued. I winced in pain, trying to protect my head, my face.

'I haven't done anything!' I cried out. 'He was the one who went back to prison!'

But her face was twisted in anger, she wasn't listening to anything I said, only intent on some kind of revenge.

Somehow I found the strength to get up. I pulled myself up from the floor, and once I was on my feet I was off, running through the house, out the door, towards the car, limping because I'd lost a shoe.

Jessie looked horrified when she saw me all battered and bleeding.

'What happened?' she said.

'Just go!' I sobbed.

Mum was equally horrified when I got home.

'Right, this is it, Adele. Ring the police,' she said, going straight for the phone.

I sat on the chair in the living room while we waited for them to arrive, an ice pack on my cheekbone in a feeble attempt to take down the swelling. Already it was impossible to see the last of my suntan under the bruises.

The police came and took a statement. They asked me why Michelle had done it, but I told them I didn't have a clue. But deep inside I knew Anthony well enough to know that whether we were together or apart he was never going to let me go to Ibiza without paying for it in some way.

After the police had gone, the phone rang. It was an anonymous number.

'Hello?'

'That was for going to Ibiza.'

Anthony.

'You fucked me over, and I'll fuck you over big time.'

And then the phone went dead.

I was scared. First the brick through our window, now I'd been beaten up by his sister.

'I don't want to make a statement to the police any more,' I told my parents.

'Adele, you've got to stand up to him.'

But I was frightened. What would he do next?

The police gave Michelle a warning for assaulting me, and put in place a harassment order which meant she couldn't come anywhere near me, or contact me. But I knew that even if she was banned from contacting me there would be others to take her place, and then there would be Anthony.

I just wanted to disappear somewhere he couldn't get me. I closed my eyes and pictured those Caribbean beaches promised by the cruise liner, the blue skies and sunshine of my holiday to Ibiza. I had to get away from Lowestoft. I had to get away from Anthony despite the fact that he was already locked up miles away from me. I had to get out of my life. And I knew just how I was going to do it.

I called up the cruise liner company that had come into college the next day.

'I'm going to London for an interview for a job on the cruise ships,' I told Mum and Dad.

They looked up, wide eyed, but excited for me.

This was going to be a new start.

Three months later, after completing my training with Carnival Cruises, I found myself on a plane flying out to Miami. The American city would be my home port for the next nine months, and I was nervous because it was daunting leaving home, saying goodbye to Mum and Dad. I had never even been on a ship. What if I suffered from seasickness? But more than anything I was excited. This was just what I needed.

I'd been so lucky to get Miami as my home port – the girl who sat next to me during the training got Southampton, so I never imagined I'd get anywhere so exotic, and then I'd opened my letter, a nine-month contract working the cruise ship *Destiny*, travelling to all the Caribbean islands. The girls who got contracts cruising to Spain and Portugal eyed me enviously.

It was going to be the most amazing adventure. And best of all, I was leaving everything – including Anthony – far behind.

I'd ignored any attempts he'd made to contact me over the last three months, focusing on the future instead of the past. And what a future it was.

The ship, when I arrived on it, was huge, like a floating city; bright, gleaming white on the outside and bursting with colour on the inside, from the neon-lit bars to the curly blue slide into one of two swimming pools on deck. Lifts whirred up and down beside me as I stood in the ship's foyer.

I sighed as I took it all in. How on earth would I manage not to get lost in this place? I felt so tiny all of a sudden. But the girls in the spa were there to take me under their wing, just like they did all the new recruits. Lisa would be 'mum' to me when I was first on board, making sure I knew what was what. But it didn't take long to make friends, not when there were so many people coming and going all the time. By the end of my first 14-hour shift, on my feet, doing massages back-to-back and selling products, I should have been exhausted, but the other girls in the spa couldn't wait to introduce me to the ship's night life.

And it was crazy: the nights after we clocked off were like one long holiday. We could drink in the crew bar for just one dollar a drink and dance until 4 am; we could go to the theatre to see a comedy show. We'd inevitably end the night lying on deck under a blanket of stars as the ship glided through the ocean, taking me further and further away from home. I could talk to boys too – I could make friends with them, I could sleep with them – and no one could check up on me, no one could say I couldn't do anything. I was 19 and doing exactly what I should be doing. It was like I was making up for every single night out that Anthony refused to let me have, for holidays where I stayed indoors. Here, all that was forgotten as we partied under the stars, and I snogged my fellow crew members, as me and my roommate Eilidh figured out who would give up their bunk bed so one or the other of us could bring a bloke back.

There were the days off too, the ones when we'd dock in one beautiful port after another and club together to get a taxi to the most beautiful bay on the island. We'd climb waterfalls in Jamaica, hire bikes and ride around Key West in Florida, swim with turtles or stingrays, wander around market stalls, or I'd Skype Mum back in Suffolk and show her exactly where I was spending my day off.

Then there were the days when we'd just stumble off the boat with a hangover and plonk ourselves in the nearest bar for the day. One, the No Name Bar in Mexico, was where all the crew members from ours and other ships met. We'd get free wifi and spend the day drinking by the pool, running across the inflatables in the water, dancing on tables. Every time we docked in Mexico I would never remember getting back on the ship at 11 pm, ready to set sail an hour later.

Christmas that year was of course spent on the boat, and

my gift was a new best friend, Hayley, who arrived on Christmas Eve from Ireland to work as one of the hairdressers on board. We bonded immediately, and the next day spent Christmas Day in Mexico under a hot sun rather than looking out of the window at home hoping for snow. As the clock struck midnight on New Year's Eve a few days later, we were gliding through the ocean. I'll never forget standing on deck as guests and crew counted down from ten to midnight, and how the black sky was suddenly filled with fireworks and we all jumped up and hugged and kissed.

And in that moment I was reminded of another New Year's Eve – the one with Anthony – and it only served to remind me just how far I'd come, but it also brought tears to my eyes. I sank down on an abandoned sunbed and sobbed.

Hayley and Eilidh were soon at my side. 'What's wrong?' they asked.

'I'm happy,' I told them as they wiped away my tears. 'I can't believe how much my life has changed, it's amazing.'

And it was. I couldn't remember the old me, the one constantly walking on eggshells, afraid to go out with her friends and always apologising for something I hadn't done. Here I'd spent months having my hair dyed blonde, each pack of foils that Hayley had applied in my cabin turning me that little lighter, deleting the old me, the brunette who was controlled by my ex-boyfriend. Here I'd been reborn, like a butterfly emerging from a chrysalis. My transformation was now complete, and maybe that's what was making me cry, looking back at just how far I'd come.

'Well, if you're happy then stop crying!' they said, and we hugged in the middle of the Caribbean Sea.

It was nights like that when I'd call home, drunk and happy, but missing my mum and my best friends. I knew the time difference well enough to know that at 2 am they'd just be getting up for work, and I'd think, *Let's give them a drunken wake-up call*. I could always close my eyes and picture Mum's face as I told her, among the whoops and the music and the chatter from my friends, just how much I missed her.

I didn't need to wait long to see her, though. A week after my twentieth birthday, she and Dad came out to cruise for two weeks. Hayley's mum came out the same fortnight, and the pair of us spent every free minute we had hanging out with our families.

One night, long after they'd gone to bed, we ended up drinking with the Italian boys who helped sail the ship. Back at their cabins, we each fell asleep in their bunk beds. It wasn't untypical for the alarm to go off at 7 am and we'd wake up with a start, after just a few hours sleep, wondering who we'd been with and how we'd get back to our cabins to get ready for work at 8 am. That morning, Hayley and I giggled to ourselves as we wandered through the corridors back to our cabins from our two Italians. But we turned the corner just in time to find our mums standing outside our doors. They looked us up and down, not missing the fact that we were still dressed in last night's clothes.

'And where have you two been?' Mum said, folding her arms, as Hayley's mum tapped her foot.

Our blushes probably answered their question.

I didn't miss Anthony while I was on the ship – why would I? Not that I didn't think of him. I'd heard from my friends that he was out of prison, and as the date before the end of my contract approached I tried to get Eilidh to add him on Facebook, just so I could suss out where he was, what his frame of mind was. But he didn't accept her.

'You've got to promise us you won't go back to him when you get home,' Hayley said one night as we sat drinking.

'Of course I won't! Everything is different now. I'm different now.'

I knew I was better off without him, I couldn't imagine a time when I would go home and put myself through that again. I'd already proved to myself I didn't need him.

The day before we docked back in Miami and prepared to leave the ship, Eilidh and I spring-cleaned our cabin ready for the next crew members who'd share it. As we did, we were in tears. I didn't want this adventure to end.

'I'm coming back on the ships in three months,' I told her. 'But Amie is pregnant, she's due in a few days. I just want to go back and be there for her when she has the baby.'

'Well, make sure you do come back,' Ellie said. 'This ship has been the making of you.'

And even though she hadn't seen the old me, the one controlled by Anthony, she had no idea just how right she was.

I hadn't told Mum and Dad I was coming home when I did. Instead I surprised them by just walking in through the front door one afternoon to their utter surprise and delighted cries.

'We weren't expecting you for another week!' Mum said, jumping up from the sofa. 'Look at you, you look amazing!'

I knew what they meant: I was blonde and tanned, happy and excited to be home.

'I want to go out with my friends tonight,' I told them as we all had a cup of tea. 'I've missed everyone so much.'

'Of course!' Mum said. They didn't mind that I'd only been home five minutes and I was off out, they knew I'd missed my friends, not only when I was on the cruise, but before, when I should have been going out with them, doing what every teenager does.

That night it felt great to be back upstairs in my old bedroom, curling my new short bob under with my tongs, and applying thick mascara to my eyes.

Pretty much everyone who I bumped into in town that night had the same reaction. 'Wow, Adele! You look great!' And I felt it.

I would be lying if I said that Anthony didn't cross my mind, that if I spotted someone on the other side of the pub, with that same mousy hair, that I didn't feel my heart pound in my chest a little harder, but not because I *wanted* it to be him, perhaps because I didn't know what reaction I'd get if I did. Would he be as pleased to see me as everyone else? Would he notice the transformation I'd undergone? I didn't know if I wanted him to or not; all I knew was that life without him had been good, that it had afforded me a different view of the world, one that was filled with different places and people, and it had changed the way I looked at my home town.

'What are you going to do now?' the girls asked after I'd told them all the stories of life on the cruise ships.

'I'm only back for three months,' I told them. 'I've just come back to be there for Amie when she has the baby and then I'm going back.'

'Good for you, Adele,' one of them said. 'I wish you'd pack me in your suitcase!'

I looked around at the familiar pub, filled with people I recognised, and it suddenly seemed like such a small world I'd been living in, compared to life on the cruise ships.

We had a great night, it was so good to see the girls, so when they called last orders I wasn't ready to go home.

'Let's go to Hush,' someone suggested.

We all piled into the nightclub, checking our coats and heading to the bar. The music was pounding in my ears, pumping in time with my heart as I followed my friends up the stairs. I glanced down in the club at everyone dancing, or standing on the edge of the dance floor, this old place still the highlight of their Saturday night, when I'd seen so many different places and things. I was lost in that memory when I felt someone, a faceless person, heading down the stairs in the opposite direction and then grabbing my hand.

'Adele?'

I spun around. It was Anthony.

We paused there on the stairs while his eyes scanned over me, taking in the new confident me. For a moment I could see he was speechless, but then his face broke into a huge smile.

'Oh my God, I can't believe it's you!' he said.

For a second I could have relented, I could have allowed his smile, that glimpse of the man I'd once loved, to let my guard down, I could have been friendly. But instead, bolstered by alcohol and my friends around me and my new confidence, I shook my hand out of his.

'Anthony, I don't want to speak to you, go away.'

Instantly, he looked stung.

'Adele,' he tried, reaching for my hand again. 'Let me speak to you. We ended so badly, I –'

'Anthony, fuck off, I want nothing to do with you.'

And I hurried up the stairs to join my friends, my heart racing inside my chest.

He followed me up there, he tried again. I turned my back on him, but still he went on and on.

'Just leave me alone, I'm with my friends!'

Eventually, a bouncer must have noticed what was going on, because before I knew it he'd stormed over, and was leading Anthony away.

The look on the faces of the other girls was relief, but inside I suddenly felt frightened. I'd only been back one day and already I'd got Anthony kicked out of a nightclub. This wasn't what I wanted to happen.

'Come on, have a drink,' Remi said.

But it was suddenly hard to concentrate: the music was too loud, doing little to block out the memory of him as the bouncer led him away.

A few moments later two girls came up to me.

'Anthony's outside, he just wants to speak to you, Adele,' one of them said.

I looked at my friends. The look on their faces was enough to tell me they didn't want me going outside to speak to him.

'He doesn't want any shit,' the other girl said. 'He just wanted to know how you're doing.'

I sighed then because I knew Anthony, and I knew that unless I said yes, unless I went to speak to him, there was no night for me, there was no reunion with my friends. Not unless he got what he wanted.

'OK!' I said eventually. 'I'll go and speak to him.'

'Adele!' I heard one of my friends call after, but I was already striding towards the doors of the nightclub, my chest puffed out, drawing on my new confidence. I could do this, I could speak to him and, better than that, I could tell *him* just what a great life I had now. I looked good, I felt good. I could be in control now.

He was waiting outside, his face creased into a smile when he saw me. He outstretched his arms and wrapped them around me, squeezing me so tight that it took the breath away from me, and with it, a little of my guard. I felt in those arms, in that hug, everything that he did. I felt how much he needed me, wanted me.

'Oh Adele, I've missed you so much.'

It was so heartfelt, so full of longing. So genuine.

But everything was different now, I was different … And then I felt his lips on mine, a kiss that told me everything he still felt about me, and for a split second I found myself melting into it …

'No Anthony!' I said, pushing him away. 'We can't do this, not any more, not ever. I'm over it!'

'I just want to talk to you, Adele. We went through a lot together. I want to know you're OK now –'

'I'm fine,' I said. 'I'm brilliant. I've got a boyfriend, an Italian guy, I'm going back on the cruise ships, and he's going to be on the same one. I've been all over the Caribbean, I've met so many different people, I've had such a good time …'

On and on and on I went, and every time I paused for a breath he tried to tell me something about himself.

'I've got a baby on the way …' he tried.

'I'm happy for you,' I replied.

And still I went on, telling him what a great time I'd had travelling the world. It was a competition between us that he could never win, his experiences in his small town could never match mine, and I wanted him to know that. And when I was satisfied that me and my new life had made him feel as small as I possibly could, I turned to go back into the club.

'I hope your baby keeps you out of prison,' I said.

And that was it. Or so I thought.

But of course it wasn't. I woke up the next day to messages from Anthony on Facebook.

You looked so amazing xxx

> Anthony, I don't know why
> you're still speaking to me.
> We're over.

Just meet me. Xxx

> No.

Meet me, Adele. Xxx

I want to make it up to you,
I never thanked you for
everything you did for me, I
only ever treated you like
shit. Xxx

Meet me. Please Adele. Let
me take you out for dinner.
Xxx

Perhaps, as the days went by, it was because I was grateful of the attention, perhaps I was simply bored, but one day I found myself typing out a reply to him.

Ok. Outside of Lowestoft
though.

I didn't want anyone seeing me with him, I didn't want anyone to know that I'd agreed to have dinner with him. But that's all it was, just dinner. I was in control of what happened now, this new confident me, the blonde girl with the tan. The one Anthony thought looked so amazing …

He picked me up at the end of my parents' road, and we drove through country lanes one June evening to an out-of-the-way pub. However much I thought I'd changed, though, Anthony had changed too. Before he'd only ever talked about himself – he was never interested in me or my life – but now he listened, really listened.

I didn't hold back any of the details, I told him everything about the cruise, how we were in and out of each other's cabins, I wanted to see him squirm when I told him about the men I'd met. But he didn't.

'I'm pleased for you, Adele,' he said. 'You've really made something of yourself.'

'Oh …' I said, so I went on some more, perhaps I wanted a reaction, perhaps that flash of jealousy that reminded me that he still wanted me. But even when I told him about the Italian guy I'd met – not that he really was a boyfriend – Anthony didn't flinch. He was so different. He was the relaxed guy I wish I'd known. The same Anthony but without the edge, without the anger. We actually had a good night, we laughed, we talked about the old times; he reminded me of the good times.

'We can't keep doing this though,' I said, as he picked up the bill. 'But if I see you around, it would be nice to say hello.'

'Yeah,' he smiled. 'That would be good.'

'Because I'm so over you now,' I laughed, joking … half joking.

He laughed.

When he dropped me off near home, he didn't try to kiss me or hug me as I got out of the car. Instead, as I left, it seemed to me that he'd finally realised what he'd lost, and he was sorry.

I lay in bed that night at home then reached over and checked my messages yet again. Nothing from Anthony.

A few days later, Amie went into labour. She called me from the hospital: she needed me with her. The only person I could call to give me a lift was Anthony.

'Sure, I'll be straight round,' he said.

A few nights later I was bored at home, stuck between Mum and Dad on the sofa.

I want to go to the cinema, I texted Anthony.

He was outside mine ten minutes later to take me there.

It was all harmless, I was going back on the ships in a couple of months after all, and the difference was that this time I was in control. So when we kissed after another night out, when he suggested we got a hotel together, when we made love, we did it because I was in charge. This time I knew what I was doing. He was different. I was different.

We'd both grown up. I could handle myself. Everything was different after the ships, but I'd realised one thing remained the same.

I still loved Anthony.

CHAPTER 6

BLAME

We had to sneak around at first, which probably added to the
excitement of our reunion. We knew nobody would approve
of us getting back together; my parents would be furious, and
his family wouldn't think much better. They'd each heard so
many things about us that they'd decided that we were bad
for each other. But they didn't understand, they didn't know
what we had, they couldn't see into the hotel rooms that
Anthony booked for us; if they had they would have seen us
snuggled up under the duvets, or holding hands while we
watched a DVD, or laughing together, or kissing each other,
or talking until the sun broke through from a night sky, and
only then falling asleep in each other's arms.

Those were the times when life was perfect, when I knew
why I'd gone back to him, it was simply because I couldn't
live without him. I'd tried and he'd pulled me back in, from
that first tight hug outside the nightclub when I'd resisted so
hard not to let my body melt into his. But I hadn't tried hard
enough, had I? Because deep down I still loved him, and he
still loved me. After everything we'd been through, that had
to mean something, didn't it? So that's how it was – me and

Anthony against the world. I knew Anthony was different now, he'd even got a job labouring and was living back with his dad, but keeping our relationship secret was expensive, so he had to use his wages to buy us nights in hotels so we could be together. Because that was all we wanted, just to be together. After all that time apart, after we'd proved everybody wrong, didn't we deserve that?

If only it was always like that, if only I could just keep the good bits of Anthony. But that wasn't how it worked, I'd known him long enough to understand that. But this time I tried not to take the bad bits too seriously, to just know that it was Anthony, that the next day he'd be sorry for whatever he'd done or said. But the problem was, every time I got used to the new set of rules he'd made, he'd change them all over again, and before I knew it I'd broken one that I didn't even knew existed.

'You don't really need Facebook, do you?' he said, one day while I was checking it.

'Yeah, it's how I keep in touch with my friends from the cruise ship,' I said.

He looked over again. 'But you got rid of it before.'

'But you've got Facebook,' I reminded him.

'Yeah well, I need it. Your real friends keep in touch with you without Facebook.'

I logged off from my account. It was easier than sitting here listening to him moaning about me being on it.

When I did, though, he started looking at his own Facebook account on his phone.

I said nothing. That was Anthony, a contradiction. One thing you could say is that life was never boring with him.

It wasn't like we didn't still argue, though, but that was just part of our chemistry. If we'd had a row and I wouldn't answer the phone to him he'd send me a text threatening to go round to my parents. He knew that always made me get in touch, the fear of him taking our problems to their door.

And he was still a pain, he did pester me. If I didn't fancy going out one night, he'd just go on and on until I gave in. If I didn't, he'd tell me he was coming round to my parents' house to pick me up.

'You know you can't come and pick me up here,' I'd say.

'So come and meet me, or I will.'

I sighed. But I did.

If we thought we were fooling people, it didn't last long, though.

'You're back with him, aren't you?' Mum said one morning when I got home from a night at another hotel.

I wasn't going to lie to her.

'I love him, Mum.'

She sighed.

'Adele, what are you doing wasting your life with someone like him? Think about your year on the ship: you were a different person, you were happy.'

'I'm happy now,' I told her.

'Hmmm, for how long?' she muttered.

But I didn't care what she said, or anyone for that matter, because I believed in Anthony. I knew I hadn't been wasting my life with him, the fact that we'd got back together again just proved that. Why couldn't everyone else see that? Yes, Anthony had pestered me back into this relationship, but only because he knew – just like I did – that we couldn't leave each other.

But this time it was different, because now I was a different person, I was strong, I was blonde, he couldn't control me any more. We were equals.

'Don't bother putting all that make-up on,' he'd tell me in the morning when we were getting dressed.

'I like putting it on,' I told him.

'You don't need it, you're beautiful without make-up.'

I put my lipstick back in my make-up bag. Maybe I didn't need so much make-up just to go out in the day.

'And I don't know why you're keeping your hair blonde,' he said.

'Everyone else says it looks good.'

'Yeah well, I hate you blonde, you look better your natural colour.'

'But I like this.'

'Well, I'm just telling you what looks best, Adele, and you don't suit blonde.'

I turned back to the mirror, my hair-straighteners in my hand; then I went to plug them in.

'Come on, there's no time to do your hair. Just keep it like that, it looks fine.'

'But it doesn't, Anthony, it's a bob. I need to curl it under.'

'No you don't. It's fine.'

So my straighteners went back in my bag, because he insisted we were late leaving the room.

But things were still better now. I stuck up for myself, I wasn't pushed around by Anthony. And then I'd catch a glimpse of my reflection in a window on the way out of the hotel; hair unstyled, no make-up. How could he say I looked better like this? I didn't look like the smart girl who'd returned home from the cruise.

I still arranged to see my friends though.

'You didn't tell me you were going out with the girls tonight,' he said.

'I did,' I told him. 'You must have forgotten.'

'It's just I had something planned for us tonight. I've booked a restaurant, thought I'd take you out for dinner, surprise you.'

Suddenly, I felt guilty that he'd gone to all that effort.

'But I said I'd go out with them.'

'Oh Adele, we've only just got things on track, don't let them ruin it all.'

So I cancelled them, and instead got ready to go out with him. But when eight o'clock came around and he hadn't come to pick me up, and then nine, and then ten, I called him.

'Sorry babe, I got drinking with the lads,' he slurred.

'But you said we were going out, and why are you drunk? You know I hate you drinking!'

We rowed, I hung up, too angry to call the girls now. Not so much with Anthony, as myself. How could I have let him do that to me again? Why did he always manage to manipulate me into doing what he wanted me to do? What had happened to the strong Adele who had come back from the ships?

She was lost at sea.

* * *

In August 2012 we'd been back together almost two months. It was a hot, sunny day and I'd spent the afternoon with Amie and her new baby, Harry, down at Oulton Broad, a local park. Anthony had rung me asking where I was and saying he was drinking on the beach with the boys.

'What are you drinking for, Anthony?' I asked. I could tell he'd had too much already, and more than anything I was worried. I knew that when he was drunk he was capable of anything.

We argued and I hung up, and then he texted me back a few hours later to tell me he was at the Wherry Hotel in Lowestoft.

'Come and meet me here,' he said.

Amie wanted to take Harry home, so I went off to meet him. I knew I'd be angry with him, though – he knew I hated him getting drunk – but I wanted to be there. At least if I was there he wouldn't get into any trouble. I could keep him calm.

When I arrived at the hotel he was sitting in the bar with two of his friends, Glen and Scotty.

'Anthony, why are you drinking? I hate it when you're drunk.'

'Oh come on, baby, just sit down, get a drink.'

'No,' I said, yanking my arm out of his hand. 'You tell me you won't go out and get drunk, but here you are. Why do you do it, Anthony?'

We argued, and eventually he understood that I was just worried about him.

'Look, shall we stay here tonight? I'll leave the boys now and we can go upstairs and chill out.'

I nodded, and waited for him while he went to book a room.

'Come on,' he gestured, leaving the boys.

We hadn't been up there long, though, when he looked at his phone.

'I need to nip downstairs,' he said. 'Scotty needs to use my phone to call someone quickly.'

I rolled my eyes and turned back to the TV. But half an hour, an hour, two hours went by and he was still down there drinking.

I jumped a little when the door of our hotel room burst open. Anthony filled the frame of the door, but he wasn't just a bit tipsy like he'd been earlier. Now, he was blind drunk. His eyes flashed green, wild and angry. I knew that look and I was frightened.

'Where've you been all this time?' I asked.

'Drinking, with my boys, and I want to know why you were such a *slut* when I was inside.'

'Anthony, what are you talking about? We've been through this, there was no one else, only you …'

He started walking slowly over to the bed. I sat up, backed away a little with each footstep he took closer.

'Come on, who was it?' he spat. 'Who were you sleeping with when I was in prison? Or maybe there were a few of them? Who was it?'

'Anthony, there was no one –'

'Liar!' he stormed. 'You're a slut, Adele. A slag. That's all you've ever been, *a lying slut*!'

He spat the words out of his mouth at me, and as he did I felt a crack at the side of my face. *Whack*. It suddenly felt like my jaw had split in two. I was on the floor in seconds, a crumpled heap, and the imposing figure of him stood over me for just a second. His fist was clenched, his fingers flexing inside his hand.

'Anthony! You punched me!' I screamed, the shock in my voice reverberating around the room.

I could hear doors opening in rooms all around us, footsteps rushing towards our room, and then I saw Anthony running away, pushing past other guests who'd come to see what was going on.

I lay on the floor in tears, in agony. He'd never hit me before, never laid a finger on me, I never thought he would, he *could*. But he had. I couldn't open my mouth, it felt like something had exploded inside my head. I gathered myself up and staggered to the bathroom, I stood swaying slightly in front of the mirror as I examined my face. There was no blood, just a bruise that was already turning purple, but it wasn't my jaw that hurt so much as my heart. Anthony had punched me. *Anthony had punched me*. My head was spinning, I needed to get away.

'Magaluf?' Mum said.

'Yeah, my friend Hayley is there, working in the bars, she's already said I can stay with her.'

'But you've only just got back.'

'I know. But now I need to get away.'

I didn't have to look up to see that Mum was studying me. If I had glanced up I would have no doubt seen the confusion stretched wide across her face, the puzzlement expressed in the criss-cross of her eyebrows. Instinctively I turned away from her, not only didn't I want her to read any signs from the look in my eyes, but I didn't want her to notice the bruising to my face that I'd managed to cover with thick foundation. But I knew that she'd already be putting two and two together and realising that Anthony had to have something to do with this. She just knew better than to ask.

After I'd staggered from that hotel room and out into the street, I'd texted my friend Paige who lived nearby, and got a taxi to her house.

'Oh Adele, what has he done to you now?' she said, laying me back on the pillows on her bed and getting me ice to put on my jaw.

'He's never hit me before,' I'd insisted, sounding like I was defending him, but more likely myself, because I'd never stay with a man who hit me. And perhaps that's what hurt so much now apart from my face, the fact that I knew Anthony had crossed a line, that we could never be together now he'd hit me.

The plan to go to Magaluf was already forming in my mind, even then. If I closed my eyes I could still remember the girl who'd returned to Lowestoft two months before, the strong and happy, tanned and ambitious person I was, someone who had grown out of the town I'd grown up in; who had met so many more people, done so many more things. And now suddenly I was the girl who let my friend apply ice because my boyfriend had attacked me in a hotel room, the girl who masked her bruises from her mum.

I'd known almost instantly that I couldn't stay in Lowestoft, not if I wanted to be free from Anthony. He'd always be there. He'd never leave me alone. And so I needed to escape, and I thought of Magaluf.

Of course I heard from Anthony as soon as he sobered up. A text.

I'm sorry Adele. xx

I don't want anything to do with you, Anthony.

He was on the phone then, begging me, pleading with me to forgive him.

'You punched me, Anthony, how can I forgive you for that?'

But he obviously thought I should because he kept ringing and begging me to. Finally, I snapped.

I'm going to Spain for the summer. That's it. We're over.

If I thought he was just going to sit there and let me go I was wrong. He bombarded me with phone calls, text messages. I ignored all of them because my ticket was booked for just three days later. In 72 hours, I'd be gone.

But then of course, when the begging didn't work, he got nasty. He threatened to ring my parents' house, to go round there, he even hinted that he'd harm them if I didn't answer his calls and texts.

Even at the airport I ignored them, though. The fact that I still winced in pain each time I chewed my food or brushed

my teeth was enough to remind me that Anthony was dangerous. I'd always been scared of Anthony, but I'd never thought
he'd lay a finger on me. And now he had. It had to be over
this time.

On the plane out to Spain, I stared out of the window.
Finally up here, above the clouds, I was free, but it was ridiculous that I had to go to such lengths to be free of this man.
He'd attacked me and I was the one running away. But if
that's what I had to do to finally get him out of my head, go
30,000 feet up above the clouds, then I would.

The only problem was that back down on earth I still had
to live with myself, I still had to ask myself why I'd been
sucked in by him again, why I'd let him convince me that we
were better off together than apart. Why did I do it to myself?
The answer came over and over again, because I loved him.
But my hand reached up to my jaw and I told myself I
couldn't, not any more.

In Majorca, Hayley was there to meet me from the
airport.

'Oh hun, what happened?' she said, wrapping me up in a
hug.

The last time we'd hugged it was saying goodbye on the
cruise ship. Now look at the state of me, fleeing England from
the abusive boyfriend I'd promised never to go back to.

'It's OK,' she said. 'You're safe here.'

I switched on my phone after I'd left the airport, and there
they were – dozens of texts and voicemails. I hadn't had it on
five minutes when it started ringing. He was even trying to
get to me here, and emboldened by the friend I had at my side
I finally snapped.

'Anthony, you've got to leave me alone. I'm in Spain now, I've left. Just leave me alone.'

But the small voice on the other end seemed shocked to have heard an international dial tone.

'You've really gone?' he said. 'You went to Spain.'

'Yes, because you punched me, because it's over between us.'

'Don't say that, Adele,' he said. 'You've got to come back, you've got to get back *right now*.'

'No, Anthony! You're not telling me what to do any more!'

I put the phone down, the fury coursing through me. It rang again, I answered, if nothing else to tell him to get away from me.

'You're the girl I love, Adele. My head's just messed up. I always hurt the ones I love.'

'I don't care, Anthony. I don't want to hear it.'

I hung up, again. And then a few minutes later my phone rang again.

On and on and on it went all day. Hayley and I left the airport and headed to her tiny apartment in Magaluf. My phone was still ringing inside my bag. Each time I glanced at it there was a new text message.

> I watched my dad hit and
> strangle my mum and I said
> I'd never turn out like him.
> I'm sorry, Adele, come back
> and I'll make it up to you. I
> love you. xx

I didn't reply.

By the time I answered it again I could tell he was drunk.

'Come back right now, Adele!' he stormed. '*Get home now!*'

'No, Anthony, I'm not coming home.'

'Then I'll kill myself,' he said. 'I'll commit suicide. Unless you come home, I'll do it. Or … or … I'll go and stab your parents. I'll do it, Adele, unless you come home.'

'Oh Anthony, shut up.'

'I'll do it, I'll get in my car and drive onto the train tracks. You'll make me die and then you'll have to live with it for the rest of your life. You'll have to live with the guilt of knowing you killed me.'

'You're drunk, Anthony. Leave me alone.'

I hung up the phone again, but the threats kept coming and coming until finally even my phone had had enough. The next time I picked it up the battery was dead.

'At last some peace,' I said to Hayley.

We went out that night, my first night; it felt good to be there, the warmth of the evening on my skin, the bars, the music, the holidaymakers, the fun. It was easy to forget everything then, to forget Anthony, to forget his fist slamming against my jaw, the hurt, the shock. I was a million miles away from all that.

We got back in the early hours of the morning. It was nearly 5 am, the night's sky slowly bleached by a rising sun out across the sea, by the time I started to unpack my case to get ready for bed. It was then that I plugged my phone in, and one after the other the messages pinged into it; texts, missed calls, voicemails. I charged it up enough to listen to the answerphone, and when I did my blood ran cold.

'Hi Adele, it's John, Anthony's dad, look … Anthony's been in a car accident. He had to be cut out of his car near the train station. He's in a bad way …'

'Oh God!' I cried out.

'What?' Hayley said, rushing in from the bathroom.

I looked at her, trying to find the words to speak. 'He did it. He tried to kill himself. They had to cut him out of the car. His dad says he's in a bad way. I have to get home.'

'What? Wait! Adele, no, you don't have to get home.'

'I do, Anthony's in hospital because of me. He tried to kill himself because of me. He told me he would and I didn't listen and he could have died. He might die. I've got to get a flight home.'

I was already throwing clothes back into my suitcase, intermittently throwing my hands up to my face. 'What have I done?' I cried. *'What have I done?'*

Hayley took me by the shoulders. *'You* haven't done anything, Adele. *He* punched *you.* You didn't make him do this, it's just a way of getting you home.'

'It's not,' I said. 'He's in hospital. What if he dies? What if he dies and it's all my fault.'

'It isn't your fault!' Hayley said, and then she started crying because whatever she said she could see it made no difference at all.

'Please Adele, please don't go back to him. Stay here with me. Look how he changed you, look what you've become, he's broken you. Stay here with me.'

But there was no changing my mind. I had to get back to England, to Anthony. I had to make sure he was OK.

Hayley sobbed as I called a taxi. She held onto me so tight when it was time to leave.

'Don't go,' she tried again. But it was no use.

'I'll text you when I'm home,' I said, heaving my suitcase into the back of the cab, and then I left. I'd been in Magaluf less than 24 hours, and I was on my way back to the airport. But there was no other choice, I couldn't live with the guilt of what I'd done. I had to make sure he was OK, and that he never did anything like this again. Even if it meant staying with him.

The first flight I could get out of Majorca was going to Gatwick three hours later.

'I'll take it,' I'd told the cashier.

It meant that I had to get a coach from London to Norwich, which took more than four hours, and then a bus from Norwich to the James Paget Hospital in Gorleston. I kept my phone close the whole way, calling his dad and eventually getting through to Anthony himself. He sounded weak.

'I'm so glad you've come back, baby,' he said. 'I knew you loved me.'

When I arrived at the hospital, he was outside waiting for me in a wheelchair. He looked such a sorry sight that once again guilt stung inside my chest. He was wearing the pale blue hospital gown, clutching hold of a drip at his side.

'Oh Anthony!' I said, as I dragged my suitcase along behind me. Gingerly, he stood up and I wrapped my arms around him, and despite the fact that when he squeezed me I still felt the last of the pain he'd caused pull at my jaw I closed my eyes and felt tears in them for him. What if he had died? I was well aware even then that it was guilt not love that had brought me back, but one thing I knew was that I couldn't leave him again, I couldn't risk this – or worse – happening again. What he'd said had been right, I would never have been able to live with myself.

We pulled apart and he spotted the tears making their slow descent down my cheeks.

'I love you, Adele,' he said.

'I love you too,' I whispered, because what else was I meant to say?

I wheeled him back to the ward where his family sat around his bed. When they saw me, they got up to leave.

After they'd gone and I'd helped Anthony back into bed, watching him wince as he clutched his broken ribs, he lay back on the pillows and held onto my hand.

'Promise me you'll never leave again,' he said, smiling, his eyes happy because he had everything he wanted right there in his hand. I looked at him there in that bed, such a pathetic state, and all because of me. I thought of him drunk in his car, driving towards the train tracks, and I dropped my head and closed my eyes to blot out the images.

'I promise,' I said slowly, because there was something else welling inside me to see him so happy. I tried to swallow it down, but I could taste it on my tongue: anger that I was here again, that I was agreeing to sacrifice myself to keep him – both of us – safe from harm.

He squeezed my hand and I looked up. 'I knew you'd come back for me,' he said. He stared deep into my eyes without blinking once. 'We're back together now.'

I looked into his eyes. There had been love there once; now there was just a threat.

He was the one in that hospital bed, but inside another little part of me died.

CHAPTER 7

SABOTAGE

I'd decided on red for the colour scheme for the kitchen, and I'd loved shopping around for all the bits, from scarlet coffee, tea and sugar pots which would sit on our pale wooden work-tops to the cherry-coloured drying rack on the sink. In the bathroom, I'd bought soft, stripy towels in white, turquoise and green, as well as a matching bathmat. I wanted everything to be perfect for my first proper home, *our* first home. Not that it was much to talk about. Anthony's dad had got us the place – a one-bedroom flat in a bit of a rundown area of town – but it was our first home, and I was determined to make the best of it.

Anthony had stayed in hospital for a week after the car crash, and then we'd gone to stay with his brother John and his girlfriend Leanne. I'd never left his side, fetching him endless cups of tea or fixing him food. We didn't do much all day, we just curled up together watching DVDs. Once Anthony was strong enough we had a walk round to his dad's place. Back at the flat I'd make us food, pasta or pizza, I made a roast dinner once to thank John and Leanne for having us, but what we'd really wanted more than anything was a kitchen of our own to cook in, and now we had it.

'This is a new start for us,' Anthony had said when he left hospital. 'We've both been through a lot but this is a fresh start.'

And it felt like it. I had enough money from working on the cruise ships to buy everything we needed. Anthony bought the paint and wallpaper – black paper with huge pink and white flowers that I'd chosen for our bedroom – and I paid for the hot pink duvet set to go on the bed he brought from his dad's. I topped it off with two cushions, one purple, one navy blue. It looked like something straight out of an interiors magazine.

We were getting there, slowly, but I didn't ask my parents for any help. I already knew how they felt about me and Anthony being back together, so perhaps what I did instead was stick my head in the sand. Maybe I just stopped calling so often, or stopped dropping in too much. I didn't want anyone to tell me I was doing the wrong thing because … well, because, if I was really honest, I didn't have a choice. The car crash had made me realise that I would never be free of Anthony, however hard I tried, wherever I went. So wasn't it best to stay here and make the best of things? After all, look how much he loved me, enough to try and take his own life if he thought he was going to lose me. No one could deny that.

So we stayed at his brother's place for about six weeks, before moving into our own. I tried to make him happy then; the way he winced when he got up out of bed was enough to remind me how close I had come to losing him forever. So when he complained if I was going to see one of my friends, it was easier just to cancel. Anthony was right, we'd been through enough, and his injuries only served to remind me of that.

I abandoned my idea of going back on the cruise ships, instead signing on while I looked for work in Lowestoft. It meant that Anthony and I spent every waking hour together, but it was good, we were happy, there was nothing to argue about as long as I was at his side. Well, apart from my phone.

'You didn't tell me Amie texted you?' he said one morning as I wandered back into the bedroom with two hot cups of tea.

He was flicking through my phone, checking the messages.

'Oh, didn't I? She probably didn't have much to say,' I said, shrugging it off.

'What else are you hiding from me, Adele?'

He still had hold of the phone. I could see his fingers working through the menu, scrolling through more and more messages.

'Nothing, Anthony,' I said, trying to sweep away the tension circling in the room with a little laugh. 'It was just my friend texting, honestly.'

He threw the phone down on the bed. 'Yeah, well you should have told me, we're a proper couple now.'

I picked up the phone and held it tight inside my hand.

'I know, I'm sorry,' I said.

And then everything was fine, you see? So as long as I didn't upset him, as long as I said sorry, as long as I learnt what he liked and what he didn't like, we'd be OK. So I kept my phone switched off and hidden. That way it wouldn't annoy him.

Only there always seemed to be something else. But that's normal when you move in with someone, right?

'Why are you wearing make-up?'

'I just like it,' I shrugged.

'Who are you trying to impress?'

'Anthony! No one! I just like putting it on for myself.'

'Yeah, well, you wear too much make-up, you look better without it.' He got up and starting picking up things from my make-up bag, the expensive stuff. 'You should listen to me, I'm your boyfriend after all.'

And then the blusher he'd been turning over in his hands slipped out of his fingers and shattered in a soft pink cloud at my feet.

'You don't need it anyway,' he said, walking off. 'I prefer you natural.'

I told myself it was a mistake, that he didn't mean to do it, but that day I didn't put my usual foundation on, and now I had no blusher anyway. I just made do with a bit of mascara.

'See? You look much better already,' he said.

But he was the same with my hair too. He'd throw my hairdryer across the room if I was taking too long getting ready. I cowered as it hit the wall, the hairbrush I'd been using to curl my bob under hanging limply in my hands.

'I don't know why you spend so long doing your hair anyway,' Anthony stormed. When I bought another one a few days later, he just cut up the cord.

'And I've told you I don't like you blonde, you looked much better brunette.'

I stared at my reflection in the mirror, twirling one strand of light blonde between my fingers, remembering another reflection I'd stared at on the ships after Hayley had brightened my hair with another pack of bleach foils. Back then the brunette had represented the old me – I was glad to see it go – but now Anthony insisted that blonde didn't suit me. On and on and on he went.

'When we met you were my little brunette girl,' he said.

'But I love being blonde.'

'Well, I loved your brown hair. Isn't that more important to you?'

He kept on, chipping away, each time I washed my hair or tried to style it without a hairdryer, attempting instead to tuck it under with my fingers in the hope it would stick. It never did, instead loose tendrils flicked out awkwardly. It just didn't look good any more, so the next time Anthony nagged me to dye my hair I just snapped.

'OK, I'll do it,' I said.

'Today?'

'Yes, today.'

'Good, I'll pay for it,' and he fished into his pocket, pulling out two purple £20 notes and pushing them into my hand.

We were staying at his dad's that week while he was on holiday, so while Anthony sat inside I nipped round to the hairdresser's on the corner. The new reflection that greeted me in the mirror two hours later was nothing like the one I'd got to know and love over the past year; it was old Adele, controlled Adele, it was the version of me that I'd come to loathe.

I walked back round to Anthony's dad's house and he was there waiting for me outside with a friend. The satisfied smile on his face made me feel instantly weak.

'That's better,' he said, climbing into his friend's car.

'Where are you going?' I said.

'Out.' And then he was gone, and I was left standing there in the road. With brown hair.

Anthony didn't come back until late that night, long after I'd gone to bed. I was awake in the darkness when I heard his key scratch in the door, I smelt the alcohol on his breath as he entered the room, then I closed my eyes tight and tried to steady my breathing as he slipped into bed beside me. He reached over for me, putting his hand on my hip. He whispered my name in my ear, hot bitter breath that smelt of whisky, and I kept my eyes shut, my breath slow and steady, but inside my heart was racing. He rolled over and went to sleep, and only when I heard the deep rattles of his snores did I dare open my eyes again.

Did I still love Anthony? I tried to. Did I detest him? I tried not to. I was 20, this was my life, I was just trying to make the best of it.

Come and have dinner with
us, we miss you, Adele.
Mum xx

I looked up at Anthony on our sofa, back at the flat, already the anxiety swelling inside my belly.

'Mum has invited me round for tea,' I said, quietly. 'I haven't seen them in ages.'

'Go and see them,' Anthony said, and the knot inside my stomach untangled itself.

'Oh thanks!'

'I'll go and see Dad while you're there and I'll pick you up afterwards, two hours, OK?'

I nodded, and looked down at my phone. Two hours to see my parents when I hadn't seen them for a month. But it was something. At least I was going there. I texted Mum back to tell her, pretending, as I always did, that everything was fine, I just needed to get back for something else.

'Adele, look at you, what's happened to you?'

I was sitting in McDonald's with Amie and Paige, on a rare day that had started that morning with Anthony announcing that I could see my friends that day. I hadn't realised at first that I looked any different to how they'd last seen me, not until I'd caught my reflection in the glass and didn't recognise myself for a second: dull brown hair, pale skin, no make-up. So much had changed in the last few months.

'What are you doing?' Amie said. 'You look ill, you've let yourself go.'

I might have been offended if it had come from anyone else, but I trusted Amie, despite what Anthony said to me about her.

As the girls stared at me across our French fries, I looked up at the door in time to see my brother, Adam, appearing. He looked up and saw me. Nodded a hello across the restaurant, and left. That was it, my own flesh and blood and we didn't even speak any more. I thought back to our lives growing up in the same happy family: their teasing, mum's chastising; that all felt like a million miles away from me now. I broke down.

'I don't know what I'm doing,' I sobbed.

Amie and Paige reached out and I felt their arms around my shoulders.

'Do you love him?' they asked.

'Yes. No. I don't know,' I paused. 'Sometimes I detest him.'

And it was true, I knew what he was doing, I knew how I was being controlled, but I was trying to do the safest thing for everyone. I thought back to the arguments we had, the times I tried to blot out when his eyes shone green and he grabbed me by the shoulder, shaking me because one of the girls had texted me and I hadn't told him, so he'd convinced himself I must be texting boys too. How he'd punched the wardrobe door so hard that it now hung off the frame; how he threatened to beat me to death if I pissed him off. And I knew he meant it.

'I'm trying to do everything right,' I sobbed. 'But it's never good enough.'

The girls looked at each other and sighed.

'It never will be,' Amie said. 'You've got to leave him.'

'But look what he does when I try!' I cried. 'I want to leave him but if I do he goes to my family, if I do he tries to kill himself. It's just easier to stay and try and do what he wants.'

And that silenced them because they knew I was right. I was trapped, they saw it, I saw it. There was no getting away from Anthony.

'You can't live like this,' Paige said. But no one had any better ideas.

They squeezed me extra hard when we said goodbye.

'Promise you'll let us know you're OK,' Amie said.

I promised. But it wasn't really up to me.

Is he being ok with you?
Amie xxx

That was what the text said. But it wasn't me who read it first. It was Anthony.

'You didn't tell me Amie texted you,' he said.

'Has she?'

'Don't lie to me, Adele.' He was up from the sofa in a flash, his hands squeezing so tight around my wrists that I felt the skin burn against my tiny bones.

'You're hurting me, Anthony!' I cried out, my eyes filling with tears at the pain.

'Don't give me those baby tears,' he stormed. 'Why is Amie asking if I'm OK with you? Have you been telling her our business. Have you …? *Have you?*'

'I … I …'

'You're a lying little slut, that's what you are, Adele.' He squeezed tighter onto my wrists. I tried to move back, to escape the pain, but my back was against the wall.

'Anthony, please –'

'You've been texting people behind my back, haven't you?'

'I haven't. I promise. Anthony –'

But the fear took the breath from me. It wound itself inside my neck, stealing the air inside of me, my heart beating twice as hard to try and grab some back. The tears streamed down my face as I tried to think of something, anything I could say to try and calm him down.

'Anthony, why would I want someone else? I waited for you while you were in prison. You hit me but I came back for you. I love *you*.'

And it worked, he relaxed his grip on my wrists.

'You're fucking my head up, Adele.'

'I'm sorry …'

'And now you're getting other people involved in our relationship.'

'I'm not, I'm sorry.'

'Why does Amie need to know about us? This is our relationship.'

'I know. She doesn't. I'm sorry.'

The calm had returned to my voice, the fear abated for another day.

Perhaps he was right; perhaps I shouldn't have told Amie. Look how angry it had made him, and if I hadn't then he'd be OK right now; he wouldn't have grabbed my wrists, he wouldn't have got so worked up. He sat down on the sofa.

I bent down and wrapped his head in my arms. 'I'm sorry, Anthony,' I said.

And I meant it.

I wasn't allowed to have a Facebook account like the rest of my friends, so it was Paige who told me about the party up in Burnley. Lorien, one of the girls from the ship, was having a twenty-first birthday party, and we were all invited. Hayley was going to be there.

Me and Anthony were walking his dad's dog when Paige called to tell me about it.

'Oh my God, it sounds amazing!'

'You've got to come,' she said. 'It's going to be great!'

I looked over at Anthony.

'Er … I'm not sure,' I said. 'And I saw Hayley in Magaluf not long ago, plus Emma won't be there, and it's a long way.'

Anthony looked up at me, his curiosity piqued.

'What was all that about?' he asked when I hung up.

'Oh, there's a ship reunion for one of the girls' twenty-first birthday. I really want to go, but it's in Burnley.'

He walked on with the dog.

'Well, you've already said no.'

That was it, end of conversation.

But as the days and weeks went on I kept thinking about the party, about the chance to see all my friends from the ship. And when Emma was sent home from the ships early because her wrists had swollen, and it meant she was going to be at the party after all, my mind was made up. I remembered the person they'd last seen, tanned and blonde, and although I might look different I knew I was still her inside. So, emboldened by the memory of this confidence, I decided to speak to Anthony.

'I want to go to the party,' I told him.

'But you already said you're not going.'

'I know, but that was before I knew Emma was going to be there.'

He sighed.

'Who is this Emma?'

'She shared a cabin with Hayley. Honestly, Anthony, I want to go, these girls were there for me when we were apart, they were my best friends when I needed them …'

He looked at me. 'You're not going.'

But I went on and on, so much so that eventually I said that if he didn't let me go I'd split up with him.

'OK!' he said finally. 'You can go, but I'll book your train ticket for you, and you're not allowed to drink.'

'OK, I won't, I promise.'

I was just so thrilled and so surprised that he'd agreed. I didn't care that he booked me a train leaving Lowestoft on a Saturday morning at 6 am, and coming back from Burnley at 6 am the following morning. By some miracle, I was going to the party – I was going to see my friends.

I had no party clothes at our place – we never went out any more – so I went to Mum's to look through my old clothes. She gave me some money to spend when I was there, probably because she could see just how excited I was.

Back at home, I tried on the dress I was planning to wear.

'Why are you dressing up?' Anthony said. 'Will there be boys there?'

'No, Anthony. It's just the ship girls.'

I did everything in my power to keep him sweet for the next two days, to avoid a row, to stop him from having any reason to blow up at me. And then, finally, the day had arrived. I packed my bag including my dress and shoes and kissed him goodbye.

'I love you,' I lied as I left, because even as I sat on the train, even as we pulled out of Lowestoft, a plan was forming in my head: I wasn't going to come home.

It took more than six hours to get there, and three changes, but it was worth it just to be away. I was so excited to see the girls, but when they picked me up from the station at Burnley I watched as, in turn, their faces dropped.

'You look so different, Adele,' Hayley said. 'What's happened to your blonde hair?'

'Oh, it got really out of condition. It was so dry it was like straw.'

She didn't say anything. Instead we got in the car and went to Lorien's house. There, I tried to ignore the fact that the other girls looked at me in exactly the same way. Instead, I decided to distract them by showing them the clothes I was planning to wear. But when I unzipped my bag and reached inside, there were no clothes inside. My dress, my shoes, they were gone. I looked inside my make-up bag, but there was hardly anything in there now. Anthony had smashed all my expensive make-up, now I just had a Rimmel mascara, not much else. My night was ruined before it had even begun. How could I think he was ever going to let me have a good time with my friends?

I dropped down on Lorien's bed and burst into tears.

'Adele,' Hayley said, putting her arm around me. 'You're not the person you were. What's happened?'

But they didn't really need me to explain.

'He's changed you so much,' Lorien said.

'Why did you get back with him?' Emma asked.

Hayley stroked my hair, asking again why I'd turned it back to brown.

'It took us ages to get you blonde,' she said. 'All that work I did on your hair ...'

'I know,' I sobbed.

'And what about your make-up? You used to love putting it on.'

'He's broken it all,' I cried.

The girls could see how upset I was.

'Come on, all isn't lost,' Lorien said. 'We can drive you to New Look, get you some more stuff.'

I shook my head. 'He'll know I've bought something, he'll search my bag when I get home.'

I thought then of the concealed zip inside my bag, the one where I kept the contraceptive pill that he knew nothing about, and even the thought of him finding that made my heart beat a little harder inside.

The girls sank down on the bed beside me.

'He's controlling you,' Hayley said. 'You've got to get out.'

Just at that moment, my phone rang.

'Hello?'

He was drunk. 'What are you up to, you slut? What are you doing behind my back?'

The girls listened to the call, and by the time I hung up they were in shock.

'You can't go back,' Lorien said. 'Stay here with me for a few days if you need to. But you've got to get out of this.'

I nodded, I knew they were right. It had taken getting this far away from him to see what had been in front of me all along. I dried my tears.

'I'll leave,' I agreed. 'Soon, I'll leave, but not now, not this weekend.'

I looked to Paige, pleading with her with my eyes to back me up. She knew Anthony better than anyone here.

'You don't know what he's like,' she told them. 'He's evil.'

Silence descended on the room, and they dropped the subject.

I borrowed make-up from Hayley, and high heels from Lorien. I wore my jeans and the same top I'd travelled up in, but I felt OK, despite the fact that everyone else in the bar was in party dresses. I didn't feel like dressing up anyway, not now.

And yet despite the fact that I'd agreed to leave him some day soon and that I could have stayed in the safety of Burnley, I still didn't dare drink. And the phone calls from him kept on coming.

'Are you drinking? You better not be.'

On and on and on until I was physically sick in the toilets, not from alcohol, but anxiety. Still he went on, drinking more and more then ringing me, demanding to know who I was talking to, what I was doing.

'I'm just with the girls,' I promised him.

But at one point when I stepped outside to speak to him, to put his mind at rest, to try and calm him down, he heard men's voices, and he went crazy.

'You're a fucking slut!' he stormed. 'I've been a decent boyfriend, I've let you go to the party, I've paid for your train ticket, and you are humiliating me, you're talking to boys!'

'Anthony, I haven't done anything. You're evil, Anthony, you're controlling me, and I hate you. You've changed me, all my friends say so. I'm staying in Burnley, I'm not coming back.'

'You've wrecked my life, you fucking slut! *You've* done this to me! This is why I'm like this!'

And just as I was about to hang up, just at the moment when I could have switched off my phone and put it in my pocket, he went on:

'I can't decide what I'm going to do,' he slurred down the phone. 'I've got two methods, either I'll kill you and do life for it, or I'll go round to your mum and dad's house and slit their throats. I'll go to prison and you'll have to grow up knowing what you've done.'

A cold shiver went through my body. He meant it. I was sure of it.

'You better come home now.'

'Anthony, it's 2 am –'

'Get to the train station now or I'm going to go round and slit your mum and dad's throat. I'll break the window, I'll get into their house, and you won't be able to stop me unless you get to the train station. *DO IT NOW!*'

I went back inside the pub, and through tears that were streaming down my face I said goodbye to my friends.

'Don't go!' Hayley begged me. 'He's not here, Adele. He's miles away.'

'But he said he'd kill my parents.'

'Ring the police,' they said.

But I refused. 'I've got to go, it's the only way he'll stop.'

The girls were in tears as they put me in a taxi.

'It's 2 am, it's raining, there aren't any trains. Stay here, Adele.'

'I've got to go, I'm sorry.'

In the cab, Anthony rang my phone again and again.

'Where are you? Let me speak to the taxi driver.'

Shaking, I handed the phone over to my driver, heard him telling Anthony we'd arrived at the station. And then he hung up. When he knew I was there, before 3 am, in the pouring rain, sitting on an empty station platform, he switched his phone off. Instead, the girls called.

'Come back,' they begged me.

'If he knows I'm not at the train station he'll do something to my parents,' I told them.

So I sat there, shivering and sobbing in the darkness, waiting for my train to arrive at dawn.

The next day was a Sunday, so the train took longer than on the outbound journey. Each second, each minute, each hour, I sat clutching my phone, my mind replaying the events of the night before like some horrifying reel going round in my head. How had this happened to me?

By 11 am, five hours after I got onto the train, Anthony rang.

'What time does your train get in?'

I could tell he was still drunk. I told him, 3 pm.

'I'll be waiting for you outside Lowestoft,' he said, his voice a low growl. 'Then I'm going to drag you off to the flat, I'm going to lay you on the bed, slit your throat open and then beat you to death. How does it feel knowing that today is your last day?'

I said nothing, just felt tears making their slow descent down my cheeks and pooling in my lap.

He kept ringing back, I answered the phone with shaking hands. He repeated his threat, each time it got a little worse, telling me how he was going to kill me, how I'd pushed him to it. I believed him, that's what absolutely terrified me, I believed that this time he would kill me. So I had a choice, I could either go and meet him at Lowestoft, try and calm him down like I had done so many times before. Or I could get off at Oulton Broad, the stop before, and call my mum, tell her everything.

I dialled her number.

'Anthony is saying he's going to kill me, Mum. You've got to come and get me.'

'What?' She had just been serving up a Sunday roast for my dad, my brother, Adam, and his wife, Sarah.

'There's no time to explain, just please come and get me!'

Seeing the familiar green Renault Clio pulled at my insides as I walked out of the station to safety.

'Adele, what's going on?' she asked me when I got in the car, shaking.

'Just get to the police station,' I told her. 'Once he knows I'm not on that train at Lowestoft he'll come looking for me at your house.'

'Adele, calm down,' she started.

'Please, Mum, just drive!'

But she didn't drive to the police station, she was driving to her house. We pulled up outside.

'Mum –'

'I'm going to get your dad,' she said, unbuckling her seat-belt and ignoring my desperate pleas.

Seconds later, Dad came running out of the house.

'Adele, what's going on?' he said.

'Just get in the car!' I screamed at my parents, my terror obvious.

They did as I said and we sped to the police station. I knew by now that the train would have arrived at Lowestoft station, that Anthony would realise I wasn't on it. Now what would he do? I had to make sure that my parents were safe. That he couldn't get to them.

Finally, we arrived at the police station, but just as we sat down with an officer, just as we started to explain everything,

Mum's phone rang. I watched helpless as the look on her face turned to horror.

'What! *No!*' Mum shouted.

My heard was thumping in my chest. *What? What's happened?*

'It's Anthony. He's got into the house. He's got Adam by the throat,' she said.

Suddenly the room was spinning. Adam? No. I didn't think of Adam. I'd only thought of protecting my parents. I knew just how crazy Anthony was, everything I'd done to protect my family, and now it had come to this. What was he going to do now? Kill Adam? I had no idea. But something told me he was capable of it, and just the thought of that made my blood run cold.

Dad stood up. 'We've got to do something,' he said. 'He's got Adam!'

The police officer gestured quickly for him to sit.

'Sit down, Mr Bellis, we'll send our officers to sort this out –'

'But he's in our house!' Mum was hysterical, and then Dad was up again, pacing the small interview room, and all I could do was put my head in my hands and sob because I was terrified. For Adam. For my parents. For myself. Was Anthony going to do to Adam what he'd told me he'd do to my parents and me? Was he going to slit his throat? I closed my eyes and was bombarded with a thousand horrifying images. Not Adam, no.

Mum was desperate, pleading with the officer to do something, anything. 'He's got Adam! He's going to kill him for all you know! Do something!'

'A unit is on the way –'

'It'll take too long for you to get there,' Dad said, standing up. 'My son might be dead by the time you get there.'

Mum's hands flew up to her face at the horror – the reality of what he was saying – and I sat there, terrified, among all the chaos. What was Anthony going to do? What had I involved my family in? Did he have a knife? Would he use it? Was Adam dead already?

Oh God, what was happening?

The police officer was radioing for help. Dad sat down, stood up, none of us knowing what to do, all of us feeling helpless.

'Mr Bellis –'

'That's my son he's got!'

But there was nothing we could do but sit there and wait for the police to get to our house. The officer convinced Dad he wouldn't get there any quicker. So we waited. And waited. I sat there listening to Mum's pitiful cries, watching Dad wipe his face with his hands, pacing the room. I saw – I felt – his utter helplessness in that moment.

And then, after what felt like forever, a crackly sound came through on the officer's radio. A message: they'd got to the house, everyone was safe, they'd arrested Anthony.

'Thank God for that,' Mum said, breaking down again, the sound of her sobs mirroring my own.

We were all safe. For now.

* * *

Because Anthony had found the door open, the police couldn't charge him with anything more serious than being drunk and disorderly. But just knowing he was handcuffed, away from me and my family, was enough for me right then.

That night, though, I slept in bed with Mum while Dad slept in my bed. I felt pathetic crawling into my parents' bed, too frightened to be alone. This is what Anthony had done to me; this is what he'd reduced me to.

I couldn't sleep for hours, though; the minutes ticked by on the bedside table clock and the stars twinkled behind the curtains, but there wasn't quiet inside my head, instead my mind ran through everything that had happened, the image I'd conjured up of Anthony grabbing my brother by the throat, of Adam calming him down like he had told us he had. What had I brought into my family the day I had met Anthony? Tears ran down the side of my face, soaking themselves up in the cotton of the pillow, as I finally drifted off to sleep ...

It was 1.30 am when I shot bolt upright in bed.

'What was that?' I whispered to Mum in the darkness. She was awake instantly, like me sitting straight up, listening. Downstairs I could already hear Dad up and awake, switching the lights on. Then I heard it again, stones hitting the bedroom windows, one after another.

'What the ...' Mum said, pushing back the duvet.

Anthony had been released by police but he hadn't gone home, he'd obviously come straight round to my parents' house, shouting my name in the street, waking up all the neighbours.

'I'm going out there,' Dad insisted, heading towards the front door as we ran to the bottom of the stairs.

No! He couldn't.

I threw myself in front of him.

'Dad, please, you don't know what he's capable of.'

'I don't care!' he stormed. 'He's not doing this to my family!'

'Dad! No!' I was on the floor, at his knees, holding on to his legs, anything to stop him from going out there.

'Don't, Kevin,' Mum said. 'Look at her, she's terrified. And she's right. Anthony's crazy, he could have a knife on him.'

He looked at us both for a moment, pleading with him, then sighed and instead reached for the phone and dialled 999. Within minutes I saw the reflection of blue lights piercing the darkness. I didn't watch as they arrested Anthony. Instead I went back up to the safety of my parents' bed, burying myself deep underneath the duvet.

The next day, Adam got some CCTV from work and fitted it at the front and back of the house. As I watched him and Dad drill the lights and cameras up and down the garden I wondered how things had ever come to this. But it was a good job we had them because just a few hours later, as soon as night fell, I recognised a figure on the CCTV screens, prowling about in our back garden. Anthony. We called the police again, and minutes later a patrol car pulled up.

Every night that week it was the same; two nights later there was a brick thrown through the back window, waking us all up and leaving shards of glass scattered across the carpet in the dining room.

The following night we cowered inside as Anthony climbed on our roof extension and started stripping tiles off it.

'He's crazy!' Dad said, as we stood in the kitchen, watching helplessly as more tiles were cast into the garden below, and listening to the chaos above us. Suddenly we heard a ripping noise: something coming through the roof above.

'He must have put his leg through the bloody roof!' Dad said. He was furious, but what could he do? The police were on their way, we just had to sit tight and hope he didn't come through the ceiling in the meantime.

The police took him away again. But he was back the next night, no doubt after a day of drinking. This time Mum woke up in the night, sure that she'd heard something. It was Anthony breaking more windows but not making it through the double glazing.

Each night I cowered inside while my dad called the police. But no amount of arrests, or even injunctions, seemed to put him off. It was me he wanted after all, and I'd always known he wouldn't rest until he got me.

And then, after a week, it stopped. I didn't hear anything, there were no footsteps outside, or sounds of breaking glass, or cries of my name in the street. There was instead a few drunken texts telling me he missed me, but I ignored them all.

A few weeks later, Mum and Dad went to his court hearing for being drunk and disorderly. They sat and listened as he likened our story to Romeo and Juliet, telling the magistrate how he loved me so much, how sorry he was.

He was handed an injunction, ordering him to keep away from me and our house. Not that it worked. If I went out in town and spotted him in a club, I would leave immediately.

But he'd just follow me outside, sometimes jumping into my cab, insisting I move over and then telling the driver to take us to his place. I tried to speak up, of course I did, but I was frightened; my heart would be racing, and more often than not the easiest thing seemed to be to do as he asked, such was my fear.

One night I was out with my friend Claire.

'Why don't we go back to my place and have a drink?' she said. Her boyfriend, Zac, was there. So we did. I didn't see Anthony follow us out of the club, or jump in the taxi behind ours in the rank. I, of course, didn't hear him tell his driver to follow us to their place. The first I knew of it was, once we were inside, a furious banging on the front door, Zac opening it and seeing Anthony standing there.

'What the –'

'What are you doing here?' he stormed at me.

'I'm just having a drink with my friends, Anthony.'

'No, you're not, you're coming home with me.'

'Anthony –'

But there was no point in arguing, he'd been drinking, I knew only too well that unless I did as he said they'd be a scene. Zac looked from Anthony to me; I tried to communicate with my eyes not to argue with him. He seemed to receive my message.

'I haven't been drinking,' he said. 'I can drop you both off home.'

I think Zac hoped that if he pulled up at mine I'd just be able to get out and go inside to bed. So we set off, Anthony riding up front with Zac, me in the back. But when we pulled up at mine, I went to get out.

'She's not getting out here,' Anthony said. 'She's coming to mine.'

'No, I'm not, Anthony,' I tried.

He turned round to face me in the back, and there was a flash as his arm swept back; his fist made contact with my face. And then a short, sharp pain in my cheekbone. He'd punched me.

'Hang on a minute –' Zac said.

'I. Said. She's. Coming. Home. With. Me,' Anthony told him.

Zac looked at me. He went to speak, but thought better of it. Anthony was staring hard in his face. Instead, he put the car in gear and moved on from my parents' place.

Anthony was OK when we got home. He'd got his own way, hadn't he? Again. I was exactly where he wanted me to be. But it was just another reminder. I had to escape. I knew that the law would never be enough to keep Anthony away from me, so the next day I signed up for the cruise ships, a new contract far away in America.

A few weeks later, I was laying on a beach in Mexico under a hot sun when I got a text from Anthony.

My son's been born. This is
real love. You and me was
never love.

And it stung. Even after everything, it hurt to hear him tell me that he'd never really loved me.

> Congratulations, Anthony.
> Sort your life out for your
> son.

I got a few messages after that, each of them telling me how much better his son was than me, how much more he meant to him. I ignored them. But then the next day:

> Come home Adele, I'll
> choose you over my son.
> Let's move away, think of
> everything we had. xxx

I lay back in my cabin, in the middle of the Caribbean Sea, and put my pillow over my head. Over the next two months I'd have the same kind of messages almost every day. Would I ever truly be free?

CHAPTER 8

ANGER

Being back on a cruise ship was the best way of getting away from everything back at home, but it wasn't the same atmosphere that I remembered. I made some great friends; I met Kelly my roommate on the flight over, and Jackie turned out to be from Lowestoft too – she'd even gone to school with Adam. But it wasn't the crazy time that I'd had on my first ship: people seemed to prefer to go back to their cabins and sleep after work, and the other problem was a new rule on this ship: no alcohol for those under 21. It meant that if I wanted a night out drinking I needed to convince older crew members to buy me drinks, and that was sometimes a pain. It was still good, but I was constantly comparing it to my last ship.

'Give it a chance, Adele,' Mum said when I called her up complaining.

Things did change after my twenty-first birthday in March 2013. It was my friend Nicole's birthday too. She was a shop assistant on the ship, and we had a great night on the eve of our birthdays. When the clock struck 12 and I could officially buy my own drinks, I really went for it, dancing and doing the limbo with the guests. I got so drunk that I ended up being sick at one of the guest bars. The security guard looked the other way, knowing it was my big birthday, but I couldn't even remember getting to bed that night.

The following day we'd booked to go swimming with dolphins in the Bahamas. As I got into the water, it was the last thing I felt like doing with a hangover. But it was a great day; not many people could say they spent their birthday in the Caribbean, I told myself, and home seemed such a long way away.

The messages from Anthony had eventually abated. I'd seen how he'd changed his WhatsApp profile picture over the months. The photographs of him with his new son had stung at first – after all, there was a time when I thought that's what we'd be doing, a long while ago of course, but the memory of it still hurt – anyway, they'd quickly been replaced with pictures of him with various girls, too many to keep up with, or eventually to care about.

I'd only been on the new ship four months, though, when my contract was terminated. I was caught smoking during a safety drill. It was a smoking area and there were only crew around, but the captain insisted that me and four others left the ship at the next port. I was devastated. Even though I hadn't enjoyed this ship as much as the last, I still wasn't ready to go home.

I was nervous about returning home to Lowestoft in case of bumping into Anthony, but initially my biggest worry was what my parents were going to say to me about getting sacked. I soon got a job working as a beauty therapist at a hairdresser's in Great Yarmouth. It was a far cry from the massages and facials I did on the ship, and instead I spent day in day out waxing and painting nails, but it was a job, and being back in Lowestoft meant I got to see my friends. I made friends with two other girls at the hairdresser's, both of them called Laura, and we started going out together. I made up for the time I'd lost on the ship and when I wasn't working I was either out drinking with my friends or hungover. That's how I got chatting to Tom. He was a friend of mine on Facebook and one day sent me a message commenting on how crazy I was.

> You're either out or
> hungover! LOL!

I replied:

> I bet I can drink more than
> you though.

We started like that, sending flirty messages backwards and forwards, and then a few nights later we bumped into each other in a bar. Tom was from Beccles, about 20 minutes away from Lowestoft, and after we'd spent the night drinking together he suggested I go back to his with everyone else. We started seeing each other, but it wasn't easy as he worked nights in a plastics factory. By the following weekend when we met up, though, he had a suggestion.

'Why don't we go on holiday?' he said.

It sounded crazy – we'd only just met – but we got on, and I decided to throw caution to the wind.

'OK,' I said.

There was another part of me, though, a part that knew I was just going along with the first man who had shown me attention back in Lowestoft, the man who would mean that I wasn't known as Anthony's girl any more. So even though I knew I wasn't particularly attracted to Tom, I went along with our relationship, desperate to escape the memory of Anthony and hoping he would be the man to help me do that.

Mum thought I was mad for agreeing to go on holiday with him, but she still paid for the trip, two weeks in Egypt.

'I'm happy, Mum,' I told her. I knew that she more than anyone would do anything to help me move on from Anthony.

We had a good time while we were there: we rode quad bikes in the desert, we went on camel rides, we held hands, we slept together, but Tom never felt more than a best friend really. There wasn't that passion, that chemistry, the kind that I knew that I'd shared with Anthony.

One night we'd been out and got drunk, smoking shisha pipes in a local restaurant. When we got back to the hotel we started arguing, I can't even remember why. But something inside me snapped, a fleeting memory that flashed through my mind, Anthony bullying me, twisting my words, intimidating me. And even though Tom had done nothing like that, I pushed him away from me.

'You're just like fucking Anthony!' I snapped at him.

I didn't mean it, I knew it was the alcohol talking, I regretted it the moment I saw the hurt flash across his face, but it was too late. He walked out of the room and went and slept on a sun-lounger by the pool. The next day he wouldn't speak to me; all day he got himself drinks from the bar and nothing for me. I knew he was hurt by what I'd said, but the silent treatment he gave me only reminded me of Anthony too, how he'd made me suffer. I hated the fact that, even though I'd moved on, the memory of him lingered in every kiss, every conversation, every argument I had with any new guy I met. I'd escaped him physically, but not mentally.

Tom and I broke up when we got back to Suffolk; we remained friends but I knew I needed to be single to sort my head out.

Then, a few months later in November, I was invited to a bonfire party by another friend, Laura. She'd mentioned to me that her brother, Will, had recently split up with his girlfriend, and I'd seen him once before and thought he was nice. At the party, we ended up chatting for most of the night. I stayed with him that night, and in the morning he asked for my number.

Will was such a genuine, decent guy. He was nice looking with big, brown eyes framed by thick eyebrows that matched his dark hair. He worked off-shore so we only had time to fit in a handful of dates before he was away for three weeks. But when he came back in December he surprised me by booking a two-night break in London. The hotel he'd booked was amazing, a swanky open-plan reception with huge chandeliers shaped like giant snowflakes. He took me to Winter Wonderland where we strolled around drinking mulled wine, and then drank shots of vodka in the Ice Bar.

But there was something missing with him, something that I was used to that I didn't get being with Will. I wasn't sure what it was at first, and then, with a heavy heart, I realised:

drama. Haunted by the ghost of Anthony, I found my relationship with Will boring. I found the fact that he sent me flowers and bought me Chanel perfume and an expensive watch for Christmas cringey. I'd never been treated like that before. Sometimes, in my darkest moments, I wondered, was it because he wasn't Anthony? Had I become so used to the way I'd been treated by him that I couldn't let a genuinely nice guy into my heart? I pushed those thoughts from my mind. I hated to think what I had become because of Anthony when I was so desperate to escape the memory of him. Yet he still haunted me.

New year came around, 2014, and I broke up with Will. He didn't want things to end, but I told him we were over, and it was on that low ebb that I finished my training and started work at Hoseasons. I was desperately trying to carve out a new life for myself, but feeling like it was impossible when I was drowning in memories of Anthony.

Thud ... thud ... thud ... thud ... the treadmill shuddered under my feet, my heart pounding in my chest, trying hard to keep up the pace. It felt so good to feel the blood pumping round my body, the heat banging at my temples, my head clearing with each stride I took, and seeing the number of calories burnt make their ascent.

I loved my new job in after-sales, but the endless days sitting down at my desk instead of running around a huge cruise ship made me long for some exercise. I'd only been working at Hoseasons for a month, and I hadn't expected to enjoy it as much as I had. The work wasn't exactly exciting – dealing with customer complaints or holidaymakers wanting to change their bookings – but I loved the people, the banter, the office gossip around the water cooler.

As a beautician I'd had to get used to working alone in my therapy room, just me and my client, and often they'd drift off to sleep leaving me with only my thoughts for company. This job, though, it was more me. I did want to go back to the ships eventually, but Adam and Sarah were due to get married at the end of the year and they'd asked me to be one of their bridesmaids, so I wanted to be around for the fittings – another reason why it was a good idea to hit the gym.

Then, out of the corner of my eye, I saw a figure step up onto a nearby running machine. Red T-shirt, stocky build, the mousy hair I knew so well that gathered into a point at the nape of his neck – Anthony.

For a moment, just at the sight of him, my heart fell out of time with my feet, skipping a beat. I quickly looked away, but my hands had already given away my emotions, they were already clammy. I felt angry at myself then. How was it after all this time that my heart still leapt a little at the sight of him? How it twisted in … what exactly? Excitement? Lust? Fear? It was too hard to pick one out; perhaps it was a combination of all three. But I hated my own heart for doing it. It felt that, deep down inside my chest, it was betraying me. That my brain should override its sentimentality, by saying 'Look forward, keep running, head down.' But my heart said: 'Oh, but do you remember the time when …'

And in that instant I was back there, back under his spell, longing for the good times that had become so few and far between, telling myself that we could make it back to where we'd started if only I tried harder, or didn't let him pick a fight, or stopped seeing my friends, or calmed him down when he started drinking. But I knew also that those good times came with a price tag, and when I closed my eyes for a second, my feet finding their own way on the running machine as I did, I could still conjure up the fear, I could still see in my mind's eye the flash of anger in his eyes when he was ranting and raving at me, I could still feel the sting in my cheekbone from where his fist collided with my face.

I opened my eyes again, and glanced over at him. No one in the gym would know that now, not if they saw the two of us on our treadmills. Not unless they could look inside my chest and see the heart that both loved and loathed him in equal measure.

At that moment, Anthony looked over, and I quickly looked away. Long after I'd climbed down off the treadmill and headed for the changing rooms, I noticed my heart was still beating wildly inside.

He was there the next day again, and the next, and the next. Not only on the treadmill: sometimes I'd spot him over by the weights, other times he was on the rowing machine. If he looked over at me, I instantly looked away. I pressed the speed up on my cross-trainer, added a gradient too, anything to keep the blood coursing through me; the harder my heart worked, the more blood that I felt throbbing at my temples, the easier it was to push him out of my head.

And then, a few minutes later, I couldn't help but look over again, just to see if he was looking back at me too.

But it wasn't just in the gym I saw him. Some days I'd open the door to the sauna, a great plume of steamy air rushing out, and there I'd spot his silhouette. We'd sit alongside each other in the semi-darkness, a wall of thick steam and a wooden bench between us, the silence between us filling the air that stuck to the inside of my lungs.

And then, one day, out of the shadows came his voice.

'You're looking good, Adele.'

Hearing his voice alone was enough to make me shuffle on the bench, suddenly feeling so vulnerable in my bikini, and yet I liked what he said.

I heard my own small voice reach out in the darkness.

'Thanks. How are you doing?'

And with that we'd broken the silence between us, and I felt myself falling back into the familiarity of him. The way we could tease each other with just a look, the fact that our humour bounced off one another, the ease with which we could talk. It was easy in those moments to forget any of the horror that had come before. This wasn't the same man who had banned me from Facebook, or called me a slut time and again, or accused me of sleeping with men behind his back, or punched me in a hotel room. This was Anthony. This was a good guy. This was the one I'd fallen for. And I admit it, I liked him. I liked this version of him, not only the one I knew so well, but the one who knew me. I told myself that the other version of Anthony, the one that made fear tingle in every nerve in my body, was not the real man; after all, I wouldn't have fallen for that kind of man. No one would. No, the real Anthony was this one.

After that first day we got chatting again, I saw him more often in the gym. He always seemed to be there at the same time as me. He started coming over to chat, working out on a neighbouring treadmill. He seemed different now. Having a baby had changed him, he was grown up, more mature. The life we'd shared seemed a million miles away from this man who stood in front of me, who asked questions about my life or my job or who told me I looked fit.

'I'm proud of you, Adele,' he said. 'You've made something of your life, I always knew you could.'

I was flattered, and so I talked to him. But that's all it was. After everything we'd been through it was nice that we could be civil.

A few days later, though, he had a gift for me.

'What's this?' I asked, taking a small box from him, and opening it to find a mobile phone inside.

'I saw your screen was smashed, I thought you could do with another one.'

'Anthony, I don't want this from you … It's too much.'

'Take it, please,' he said. 'It's the least I can do after everything I put you through.'

There it was again, a reminder of the man I'd feared so much. The man he used to be. But also, some kind of apology, or at least an acknowledgement.

'Thanks,' I smiled.

'No problem.'

But I didn't know then even that small gesture would come with a price tag attached. I knew Anthony well enough to know that he didn't do something for nothing. So why had I forgotten it in that moment?

A few days later the messages started on Facebook.

Let me take you out for
dinner …

I miss you …

I still love you, Adele.

I'd open them up, roll my eyes, sigh and wonder how this had happened, how I'd got sucked back in. My head told my heart that it didn't want this, that I just wanted to be friends. And my heart said back, *You're lying*. Because I was lying to myself if I said that I wasn't just a little flattered by the attention. Life had changed since I was on the cruise ships, most of my friends had settled down and had babies now, they couldn't just drop everything and get dressed up for a night in town; instead they were at the mercy of babysitters they could rarely afford. So that left me stuck at home too. I could admit it, I was lonely, and so when Anthony asked me out I thought, what do I have to lose?

Just for old time's sake,
Adele. Please let me take
you out for dinner.

And before my head had time to protest, my heart quickly sent a reply.

Ok.

We went out for dinner a few nights later and it was everything I always knew it would be. Anthony could make me roar with laughter or giggle into my napkin. There was no sign of the old him, instead there was a man who gushed about his new baby even if he wasn't still with the mother, a man who was genuinely interested in me, who asked about my new job, who thought it was great that I was going back onto the ships.

His eyes lit up, not with anger any more but with delight when I told him about all the friends I'd made when I was overseas, about the places I'd seen. I felt safe with this Anthony, I felt my shoulders relax, I felt I could talk easily without having to search his eyes for the warning signs that he was about to flip. Or at least that's what I told myself. But perhaps I did laugh at his jokes a little too hard as I convinced myself that this time – finally – he was different.

As Anthony ordered us another drink, I fished for my phone in my handbag.

I went to check my messages and pressed the wrong button.

'Oh damn, I can't get used to this phone,' I grumbled.

'What do you want to do? Let me take a look,' he said, reaching across the table from me.

I thought nothing of him having my phone in his hands, I grumbled something about it being too difficult to get used to, how my fingers were too big for the keys, chattering away oblivious to the fact that a shadow had already passed across his face, and that a blackness had appeared in his eyes.

He spoke quietly at first. 'Why have you got boys' numbers in your phone?'

I stopped talking from across the table and looked up at him, and when I did, the food that I'd just swallowed collected in a tight knot inside my belly.

'Why. Have. You. Got. Boys'. Numbers. In. Your. Phone?'

Each word was punctuated with hatred.

'Anthony,' I tried. 'They're just copied from my Sim card … I … I didn't put them in there.'

The words stuck in my throat, I tried to swallow them down as he stared across at me from the other side of the table. I could see the whites of his knuckles as he gripped the phone. I'd seen this look before, and my body knew exactly how to react. My mouth was suddenly dry, my heart was beating wildly in my chest, my palms instantly clammy.

'Who are they?' he demanded.

'Th— they're just friends –'

'What friends? Have you fucked them? You slag.'

'Anthony! We're not even together. Just give me back my phone.'

But there was no going back, the fury had already made itself at home on his face. He wouldn't be convinced they were just friends, he pressed me more and more, calling me a slag, a slut.

'Just take me home.'

We left the restaurant in silence. He drove us home, his hands gripping the steering wheel tight, his eyes fixed on the road.

'I always knew you were a slut,' he ranted. 'Even when I was inside you were sleeping with other men. I knew it.'

I looked straight ahead at the dark night stretched out on the country roads.

'I bought you a phone and you just put boys' numbers in it.'

I thought if I just kept quiet, if I just let the miles roll by, that soon I would be home. I would be out of this car, I would be safe. My own hands gripped the side of my seat, my legs tense, wishing the journey away as he ranted beside me, the anger in his face apparent each time the headlights from a passing car cast a beam into our own. I tried to make myself disappear in that car, to be as small as possible. I looked straight ahead, detached myself from where I was. I didn't speak, because if I did, my voice would fill this small space and then he'd have something to lash out at, somewhere to direct his fury. So instead I used my silence as a shield that I prayed would protect me until I spotted the sanctuary of houses and street lights, my road, my home.

I undid my seatbelt before the car had stopped.

'You can keep the phone,' I said to him. 'I don't want anything from you.'

He wouldn't take it, he stared ahead, the anger sculpting deep furrows into his brow.

With that I was out of the car, my key was in the lock, I was on the other side of the door. My heart was saying, 'We're safe.' But my head said, 'I told you so.'

The bouquet of flowers was one of the most beautiful I'd ever seen: deep red roses and pure white lilies, and nestled among them a card: *Sorry for being a dick. I love you.*

My heart sank.

'Ooh, what a lucky girl!' the other girls in after-sales cooed.

But lucky was the last thing I felt right now, and I knew I only had myself to blame. The first thing I'd thought when I woke up that morning was how stupid I'd been, how once again I'd fallen for his charm, how once again I'd allowed myself to think that Anthony had changed. But he hadn't. Instead, when he'd started ranting, I'd heard the same excuses come dropping from my lips, explanations, reasons, anything to stop him from getting mad, and I hated myself for sounding so weak. Why had I done it? We weren't even together. In the cold light of day it was easy to see how the numbers in my phone were nothing to do with him, and yet last night I'd felt suffocated by them, I'd have done anything to erase them in that second so we could have just had a nice night. So there was nothing for Anthony to get mad about.

Today, though, I felt stronger. Today I forgot about the fear and instead asked myself why I'd made myself so small in his car, how even the breath that escaped from my lungs had felt like a trespasser in that tiny space. Today I wouldn't belittle myself, today I would tell him that he was out of order.

I picked up the flowers and stared at each and every one of their innocent petal heads. They signified much more than just the message that was carried on the card; they told me that I was back to where I started, that this was the price I had to pay for speaking to Anthony again, for taking that phone, for agreeing to dinner. He had me back.

Now, though, it was my turn to feel angry.

'Go on then, tell us,' the girls said. 'Who are they from?'

'Just some guy,' I said.

But not for much longer.

CHAPTER 9
HOSTAGE

As I waited for Anthony to come to the door, I stared at my own reflection in the glass. I was holding the bouquet of flowers, and something else, a confidence I'd found overnight. This wasn't the start of something new, it was the end, finally, and I was going to tell him that. I was sure about that. He had to know he didn't control me any more, and the only way I could show him that was face to face.

But the moment he opened the door, weakness washed over me like a wave. His eyes were wild and bloodshot, a waft of air thick with the sour smell of alcohol greeted me, and any strength I had was left on the doorstep.

He signalled for me to go inside, and I did as he said, still determined that from somewhere I could summon the strength to stand up to him. But I should have known from the moment I stepped over that threshold I was his prey.

He shut the door behind me, and my skin prickled as I heard him turn the key in the lock. My mouth suddenly felt dry as I went to speak.

'I want you to have these back,' I said, offering him the flowers. 'I don't want anything from you.'

He looked at them, and through me, then walked into the living room. I looked back at the door, and saw that he'd removed the key. Inside the living room the TV was on, and there were cans of beer on every surface, an empty bottle of vodka on the floor. I watched as Anthony picked up a bottle of Jack Daniels and gulped down a huge mouthful of it. I winced inwardly. What had I walked into?

'Sit down,' he said.

I refused. 'I just came to give you these back, I don't want anything more from –'

'*Sit down!*' he shouted.

I did as he said, not because I wanted to stay, but because I was terrified of what he'd do if I tried to leave. The terror kept me rooted just where he wanted me.

He swayed as he walked across the living room towards me.

'I love you, Adele,' he said, his breath, hot with alcohol, stinging my face. 'Why do you do this to me?'

'Do what?' I asked. 'I haven't done anything, Anthony.'

'You do it every time,' he said, holding the bottle of Jack Daniels up to his temple. 'You fuck with my head.'

I tried changing the subject. He had his suit on.

'Where are you going? I asked.

'I was going to the casino, but not now. Not now you're here. You're not getting out of this one.'

He started pacing the room, ranting and raving.

'I gave you a phone and you put boys' numbers on it!' he spat at me. 'You're a slut! You're a slut and a slag! I should have never trusted you!'

He drew his fist back and *whack*, it went straight through the door. I jumped back on the sofa, I stood up, made to go.

'Let me go, Anthony. Please. I want us to be civil but I don't want you as a boyfriend.'

But he didn't listen to me, instead with one swoop of his arm he pulled all the photo frames from the wall; they landed in a heap of broken glass by my feet. I leapt backwards, until I was against the wall.

'You've done this!' he spat. 'This is your fault for fucking my head up.'

'Please let me go,' I cried, the terror in my throat threatening to steal my voice from me.

'You're not going anywhere,' he said. And a millisecond later I saw a flash of white inside my head; it took a few seconds to register the pain that shot into my left eye. As I did, though, my legs gave way from under me and I sank to the floor alongside the shards of broken glass. My hand reached up to the pain, and as I took it away I saw the blood on my fingertips.

'My eye!' I cried to Anthony. 'You punched me!'

I started sobbing as the pain circled my head in great waves, blurring my vision and making me sick and dizzy.

'That's your fault,' he said. 'You made me do that.'

As I lay on the floor crying, I couldn't open my eye. I watched as his feet disappeared, then they reappeared with a bag of frozen peas. He dropped them into my lap.

'They're just crocodile tears,' he said, his voice frayed slightly at the edges, a little softer than before. 'Don't be such a baby.'

I put the ice-cold bag on my face, but my head was still spinning.

'Let me go, Anthony,' I pleaded. But he said nothing; he just stood over me, swigging from the bottle of Jack Daniels.

I don't know how long I was on the floor like that, but my head felt thick and foggy, and I was desperate to lay it down, somewhere, anywhere, just to relieve the pain. I stumbled to my feet and made my way, clutching the walls as I went, to Anthony's bedroom. I noticed as I did that darkness had fallen on the sky outside since I'd been on the floor. Who knows how long I'd been there?

As my head sank onto the feathery pillows, I felt some relief, but when I closed my eyes it pounded and pounded inside, the sound of my own blood banging at my temples made me want to vomit. I curled myself up in the foetal position, longing to get out, to go home. But I had no strength left in me to fight.

Suddenly I felt a warm body next to my own: Anthony's legs fitting into the back of mine, the curve of his torso, locking into my own like a piece in some horrible jigsaw puzzle. Just like we'd done so many times before, except this time I was battered and bleeding.

He pulled me close to him, his voice soft and hot in my ear.

'I want you as a girlfriend,' he whispered. 'I want to be with you, but you make me so angry.'

'But this is why I don't want to be with you,' I said, a tiny sob escaping from my voice.

He wrapped his arms tighter around my body, and my skin crawled in response. All I wanted to do was lie down, close my eyes, but instead I wriggled out of his grip. I shuffled into the toilet, but he followed me. I staggered into the kitchen, and he was there. I was crying, clutching my head. 'Just let me go!'

But the fury gathered again inside him.

'I didn't hit you that hard,' he snapped. 'Stop being such a baby.'

I would have fought him if I'd had the strength, I would have run for the door, I would have tried to get the key from him, anything, but his rage paralysed me with fear. Instead, my eyes settled on a knife behind him on the kitchen work-top, and I swallowed down more fear because I knew he wouldn't think twice about using it. In those split seconds I had visions of him stabbing me, of my cold body being found on this floor among the empty cans and bottles. I knew Anthony, I knew what he was capable of.

'Please, Anthony!' I sobbed again.

And then he was up in my face, spittle gathering in the corner of his lips as he shouted just inches from me. 'If you annoy me any more, I'll beat you to death.'

And I knew he could, he would.

So instead I tried to calm him.

'I'm here,' I said, slowly, quietly. 'Stop shouting. I'm right here in front of you.'

'You're not leaving,' he said.

'Just calm down,' I tried again.

'I'm doing this because I love you,' he said.

'If you love me, why are you doing this to me?' I pointed at my blood-stained face, the eye that I felt had already swollen too much to open.

And just when I thought I'd got through to him, just when I felt his breath calm, and the darkness in his eyes ebb away by just a fraction, he took another swig of alcohol, and started again, ranting and raving. Calling me a slag, a slut, telling me I cheated on him in prison. Each cruel word pounded inside my head some more. I closed my eyes and on and on it went.

Every so often I looked up. I watched the hours tick by on the clock behind him. When he was quiet I heard cars returning from work, people going into their homes, doors slamming, televisions being turned on, voices far from here. The moon rose through the sky, and still the hours ticked by. Five, to be precise, as Anthony went from calm to crazy every few minutes as my terrified brain struggled to keep up with his mania, just to survive. And then, in the dark of the night, the sound of an engine, a car pulling up outside.

'It's the police,' he said, sinking down onto the floor next to me. 'Hide.'

The car's headlights threw a beam through the living room curtains. The light illuminated Anthony's face. I could see he was panicking, trying to come up with a plan.

'We'll walk out together … you and me … but if you say anything to the police I'll kill you.'

I nodded. Anything to get out of here, anything to see the outside world.

So slowly I got to my feet as he unlocked the door, my heart wishing the seconds away until I stepped out of that house, and I prayed that it was really the police. But who would have called them?

As he opened the front door, I felt cool air hit my bloodied face. Freedom.

It wasn't a police car, though, it was a taxi. And Anthony let go of my hand and, as calm as anything, got into it.

And me? Finally free, I ran. I ran to Amie's mum's house as fast as I could without stopping once.

* * *

I hid for days after I got out of Anthony's house. From him, from my mum, from work. Everyone. When Amie had opened the door to me battered and bleeding, she couldn't disguise the shock on her face.

'Oh my fucking God, what's he done to you?!'

Her mum woke up and came running down the stairs, ushering me into safety.

'We've got to call the police –'

'No!' I snapped. 'I can't. He threatened to kill me.'

'All the more reason,' Amie's mum, Lynn, said.

But I shook my head, and even when I did that it hurt.

'I can't,' I cried. 'I promised him.'

It felt like my eye had exploded inside my head. I couldn't feel much of my face, my head was swimming with pain, I felt sick, dizzy, but I was too scared to get help, too frightened that a doctor at the hospital might want to know who had done this, might call the police.

'I just need to lie down,' I said, clutching the wall.

They got me a bag of frozen peas, but the ice just increased the pain. I gave up and lay my head down on the pillow, feeling it throbbing through the feathers. I closed my good eye, and felt my eyelashes wet with thick tears. I needed so much to cut through the pain and find sleep, and some peace in the safety of darkness.

When I woke up in the morning, I hoped for a split second that it had all just been a dream, but then I looked to my left and saw my smashed phone sitting beside the bed, and my heart sank. One more second of consciousness and the pain kicked in. I sat up in bed slowly, my head still feeling like it was rolling on my shoulders, making me pad tentatively towards the mirror. What I saw there took my breath away.

What was once my eye socket now bulged deep purple and black from my face, the size of a tennis ball. There was no eye, just a tiny slit, indicated only by the very tops of curled eyelashes peeking out, which marked the place where it was buried beneath. Or at least I hoped so; the pain was so bad that I feared for what was underneath all that swelling, all that bruising. And it hurt, it hurt so much. I was in agony. I clutched my head then staggered back into the bed, the softness of the duvet a stark contrast to the sharp pain thrashing at my temples.

I glanced at my phone again, but I didn't even dare pick it up, let alone turn it on. I didn't want Anthony to know that I was awake, where I was, nothing, and I knew that my phone would betray me by telling him what time I was last online, or on WhatsApp. And in that second I hated the phone for doing that, I hated the technology that allowed him to control me, to see me. I hated that small, black box for double-crossing me time and time again. I knew I'd have to turn it on soon, though, if nothing else to tell Mum I was at Amie's, but that's all I'd tell her. I wouldn't tell her about this ... I reached up and touched my face, wincing even before my fingertips found the swelling. Mum couldn't know about this; no one could.

I stayed at Amie's all weekend, then on Monday I called in sick to work. There was no point in telling them that I had a cold or a sore throat, they'd see my face before long and know I was lying. So instead I told them I'd got elbowed in the face by a bouncer while I was out at the weekend. They believed me; why wouldn't they?

When I'd turned my phone on, there were 80 Snapchat messages from Anthony. I didn't open a single one because then he'd know I was online. Instead I deleted my profile picture from WhatsApp, closed any of the accounts that would give him information about where I was, or what I was doing. I stayed wrapped up in Amie's duvet, hiding myself – and my face – from the world. Mum hadn't questioned the fact that I hadn't gone home, it wasn't unusual for me to stay with Amie, especially when her boyfriend was working away offshore.

Two days later, the thick fog that had clouded my head since Saturday night was starting to lift, so I reasoned I was well enough to go into work. All that remained instead was the sting of shame, and of course the bruise itself, despite my attempts to cover it in foundation. My Hosea-sons' colleagues were so shocked when they caught sight of me in the office.

'How on earth did that happen?' one asked.

'Have you been to the doctor's?' another said.

'It looks so painful,' someone else said.

I stuck to my story, that a bouncer had been manhandling someone out of the club and caught me with his elbow. A few people eyed me suspiciously over their morning coffee, others pressed me for more information.

'But how –'

'You should sue.'

'It looks more like a punch than an elbow.'

Again and again I repeated my story, hating Anthony even more for making such a liar out of me, before I finally sat down at my desk with an exhausted sigh.

'I know who did that to you,' Katy, the girl who sat next to me, leaned over and whispered.

I denied it of course, and I think she believed me. Only Lauren in the office knew that I'd been taking those flowers back to Anthony on Saturday night, and by the time she guessed who was responsible for it I was desperate for someone to confide in.

'Oh Adele, poor you ...' she sighed.

Just like everyone else she urged me to go to the police, but I remained convinced that if I just did what Anthony said, if I just stayed quiet, he wouldn't have any reason to hurt me again, he would finally leave me alone.

A couple of days later, though, there was no avoiding Mum any longer because it was my twenty-second birthday. She picked me up from work on the eve of my birthday, and I got into the back of the car rather than sit next to her in the front and give her chance to study my face. I had of course plastered my face in foundation, but it did little to disguise the bruises which seeped through the pigment. I also put on my glasses in the hope they might distract her, but once we were home I just took myself off to bed, and pulled the duvet up to my ears. By then, totally run down and perhaps emotionally exhausted, I'd come down with flu.

The following morning Mum came into my bedroom and gave me my presents, though thankfully she was too late for work to stay and watch me open them, and therefore didn't question why it was just the top of my head that peered out of the covers.

'I feel awful,' I said, coughing into my hand under the sheets. 'I don't think I'll be well enough to go out for dinner tonight.'

'See how you feel later ... right, I'm off.'

Once I heard the front door shut behind her, I switched on my phone, more messages from Anthony. I read one.

Happy birthday, I've got
you a present – a BMW –
it's yours if you want it. xxx

I took a selfie of my eye.

I quickly typed back, sending the photo.

This is what you really gave
me for my birthday.

Seconds later the reply came.

You did that to yourself,
darling.

Not even an apology. I sank further down into my mattress, wishing I could just hide from the world for just a while longer.

I went to work that day, and tried to be cheerful. My colleagues had decorated my desk with streamers and got me a cake; they tried to make it special for me. That night at home, the last thing I felt like doing was going out with my family. Too busy trying to hide my black eye from them, talking to them from the next room, hanging out in the doorway so they wouldn't get too close. I felt better when I was up in bed, where I could hide my face away.

Mum came up to see me in my bedroom.

'Aren't you well enough to come out to dinner?' she asked.

I sniffed under my covers. 'No, you go without me.'

'Oh Adele, we can't do that, it's your birthday!'

'Honestly, Mum, I want you to.'

There was no way I could go out with this eye looking like it did, no amount of make-up I could apply would cover it; even my glasses did little to disguise it or distract attention. In fact, Mum had even started commenting on my glasses, asking if I needed a new eye test because I needed to wear them all the time.

It took a lot of persuading, but eventually I heard the front door close behind them, and I lay up in my bedroom, tears streaming down my cheeks. Anthony was to blame for this, he'd ruined my birthday.

He didn't give up texting me. As the days and weeks wore on, he still kept pestering me, asking me to meet him, telling me he loved me. Most of the time I ignored him, sometimes I broke and that was when I sent him another picture of my face; my eye just poking through the swelling, the colour of my skin fading from blacks and purples to blues and greens.

I'd reply:

I haven't gone to the police,
just leave me alone

But the messages kept on coming. Each message that pinged into my inbox, each time my phone vibrated in the darkness on silent, made fear instantly pinch at my heart.

The fear of Anthony, of what he might say next, whether he'd be nasty or nice, suffocating me even when I was safe from him.

And still he went on.

Adele, come on, just meet
me.

Please. Meet me.

I ignored them all. But day after day after day they kept coming. It didn't matter if I ignored him or answered him, Anthony was not going to let me go.

Three weeks later, he was still begging me. Telling me in turn how much he loved me and how much I'd ruined his life. How much *I'd* ruined *his* life? Perhaps he needed to see me to see who the victim was? To see who was really suffering? So infuriated, I text him back.

OK, I'll meet you outside
your flat.

I went along in the daytime, and I had no plans to go inside. Was I afraid? Of course, but more than anything I was adamant that Anthony should see for real the damage that he had done to me. I didn't tell anyone what I was doing, because they would have thought I was crazy. I could understand that: as I walked to his house I thought I might be too. But days and weeks of hiding away had made me stronger, made me sure that this time I could handle Anthony; that this time I could keep up my boundaries, and show him exactly what he'd done to me.

As I turned into his street, he was waiting outside just like I'd asked. My heart was racing, but I was determined it wouldn't betray me deep inside my chest. He saw me and made to wrap his arms around me, but I stepped backwards. His eyes fell onto my three-week-old bruise, and tears immediately sprang to them.

'Oh Adele, what have I done?' he sobbed. Again, he reached for me, but I stepped away.

'I love you so much, I want you so much, but you just fuck my head up,' he was still crying, wiping his eyes on his jacket.

He looked so small, like a lost little boy, and that made me feel bigger, stronger, just as I intended.

'I watched my dad beat up my mum, I swore I'd never be like him ...'

'I've heard all this before, Anthony.'

The iciness I felt inside must have appeared in my voice, because Anthony looked broken, and there was a strange part of my heart, the same one that I told myself was so strong, that broke too to see him that way.

'Please don't leave me, Adele. Everyone I love leaves me, first Mum and now you. I can't live without you, I can't do it ...' and he broke down in huge racking sobs.

Instinct took over then: how could I leave him in the street breaking down like that? Of the two of us I was the stronger, I was the one who'd been beaten physically but not mentally. Just one look at the quivering wreck in front of me proved that.

'Anthony, come here,' I said, holding out my arms for him to fall into.

He relaxed into my embrace. 'Please don't give up on me – on us,' he begged.

I felt the tug of him under my skin. It was easier when things were like this, it was easier to get on with him, I wasn't scared then, I didn't need to live in fear, to dread the sound of my phone, to cower inside from him. This was easier, this was a better way to live when the other felt so … so *exhausting*.

As I stood there holding him, I found myself wondering whether I should just give up, give in to him, because it felt so tiring not to. I knew what to do: to delete boys' numbers, to not see my friends, to say the right thing. I knew the rules of life with Anthony, but did I have the energy to learn the rules of life without him? I squeezed my eyes shut and hoped I did.

A few days later, Anthony texted.

What are you doing?

> I'm going out to my friend's house

We're going to the cinema, I'm treating you

> Anthony, I'm going to my friend's

I'll be outside your parents' house in ten minutes

He knew that would work, it did every time. The fear of him coming to my family home was always enough to make me meet him.

I left with my overnight bag, determined I'd get him to take me to Kayleigh's house.

But when I got into the car, his mind was made up that we were going to the cinema.

'This is a new start,' he said. 'I shouldn't have done that to you.'

'We're not together, Anthony –' I started.

'We're going to the cinema,' he smiled. 'We can see whatever you want. My treat.'

He put the car into gear, he was relaxed, happy; those eyes I knew – and feared – were soft and twinkly, not hard and filled with hate. Maybe we could get along as friends, and didn't I deserve to be treated after what he put me through?

I sank back in the passenger seat.

'OK,' I sighed. As always, it was easier to go along with the nice side of Anthony.

And we did have a good time. We went to see *Spiderman* in 3D and before we went in Anthony raced around getting me whatever food and drink I wanted.

'Nachos?' he asked. 'Popcorn? Let's get some Ben and Jerry's too … and a Slush Puppy. Fancy a hotdog?'

'Anthony!' I laughed. 'We're going to miss the film at this rate.'

He laughed too, and we piled into the cinema, finding our seats in the darkness, his arms filled with all the snacks he'd insisted on buying.

After the film, he drove us back to Lowestoft from Norwich.

'Come and stay at mine,' he said.

'I can't. I said I'd go to Kayleigh's.'

'But it's late now.'

I checked the clock in the car, 11.30 pm, it was really too late to turn up at her house.

'OK,' I said with a yawn. I was too tired to argue with him and he was still in such a good mood. 'But I need to go straight to sleep when I get back. No funny business!'

I pointed a finger at him and he laughed as he turned his key in the ignition.

We raced back through dark country lanes, but when we got to his road he said we couldn't park outside his flat because there had been an incident with one of his neighbours that day and police had cordoned off the area.

'It's OK, we'll park at the bottom of the alley and walk through,' he said.

The alley ran the length of the houses that straddled it. It was dark, lit only by one or two street lamps. The fences that ran alongside it hid back gardens. I looked up the alley: it was only short but if I hadn't been with Anthony there's no way I'd be walking down there. A couple of bins stood outside garden gates, a black cat prowled around them, sniffing for scraps, and two teenagers exited the alley as we headed in, the smell of their cigarettes lingering longer than they did.

'Come on,' Anthony said.

Instinct told me to hold onto his hand tight. Only ten feet in, Anthony nudged me, gesturing towards one of the gardens.

'Look,' he whispered. 'There's someone over there.'

I looked hard at where he was pointing, and just made out the outline in the darkness. The figure was wearing a black tracksuit and had a hood up, a balaclava covered his face, so it was only his eyes that stared out into the night.

'Maybe he's a burglar,' I whispered back.

As we got closer, I held on tighter to Anthony, acknowledging that strangely I was safe from anyone else while he was at my side. Before I knew it, we were passing alongside the burglar. As we did, I turned to face him and those eyes followed me. I looked back at the path ahead: just a few more steps and we'd be out onto Anthony's street. But seconds later, I was aware of a scuffling. He'd jumped on Anthony.

As I turned to see what was happening, I felt a punch. I reached up to touch my face, but then it all happened so quickly. The next second the burglar was running off and Anthony was chasing after him. I watched as Anthony got him, pushing him to the ground, kicking him, the silhouettes of the two men grappling on the floor. Then suddenly I looked down at my hands, and the light from the street lamp illuminated them – they were covered in blood. My blood. I looked down at my leather jacket and saw it shimmering, wet with more blood.

'I'm bleeding! I'm bleeding! Anthony, help me!' I screamed.

Anthony came running back.

'Oh my God, Adele! You've been stabbed! Your lip is hanging off your face!'

'Ring the ambulance!' I screamed. 'Ring the ambulance!'

I was going crazy, freaking out at the amount of blood that had spilt on my hands, my jacket. I realised too that, as I spoke, my words were slurred.

I was running up and down, screaming at Anthony to ring an ambulance. But whether it was the shock or something else, he didn't do it.

'I'm ringing my dad,' he said.

And then, as I clutched my face, feeling all kinds of flesh I knew I shouldn't, I heard him telling his dad what had happened.

'Just came out of nowhere ... jumped on me ... Adele's been stabbed ...'

'Just call the ambulance!' I screamed.

Finally he hung up and did as I asked. Minutes later I saw the flash of blue lights, heard sirens. Two police cars and a paramedic.

They helped me into the ambulance while Anthony told the police officers what had happened. He followed me into the ambulance, sitting down on a chair.

'Adele, your face,' he said. I could tell by the amount of blood I was covered in that it was serious. And then Anthony looked down at his foot.

'He got me too,' he said. There was a small amount of blood on his trainer, a hole where the knife had gone in. He hadn't realised until then.

At hospital the police took photographs of my injuries. A six-centimetre gash stretched from my lip all the way down to my chin; it had cut deep through the skin and muscle, leaving the flesh hanging down my face. It was horrifying.

'I'm going to be scarred for my brother's wedding,' I sobbed, but my words just came out as a mumble as by now the pain had kicked in and along with the flesh hanging off my face I couldn't form what I wanted to say properly.

The police interviewed us both. Anthony did all the talking, telling them exactly what had happened. He was holding my hand the whole time.

'I'll protect you, Adele,' he said, over and over.

'Have you got anything to add, Adele?' an officer ask.

'She'll tell you the same as I did,' Anthony said. 'He just came out of nowhere.'

The officers looked from us to one another.

'We'd like to speak to Adele on her own if you don't mind,' one of them said.

There was something slightly different about Anthony then, the way he shifted in his seat. 'Just tell them what you saw, Adele,' he said, as he left.

I nodded – what else would I do?

But when the police interviewed me alone, I realised what their suspicions were.

'Anthony says you're his girlfriend.'

'We're just friends,' I said quickly.

'Do you think he was involved in what happened?'

'No! He got jumped on … how could he? We were together the whole night, he didn't use his phone once, he didn't even know which film we were going to see, what time it ended. How could he be involved? We had a really good night.'

The officers didn't seem convinced. But I was: this was nothing to do with Anthony. He'd been in a great mood all night, there wasn't one bad word exchanged. It was a random attack.

'Maybe we interrupted a burglary?' I offered. 'Perhaps he didn't want us to identify him?'

Once the police had finished interviewing us, they took my clothes and my phone for forensic examination. The doctors put in some temporary butterfly stitches, but I'd need an operation with a plastic surgeon. For that I needed to be transferred the next day. I panicked. I didn't want to go home, I wasn't ready to explain to Mum and Dad why I was out with Anthony.

'I can take her to mine,' Anthony said to the doctors. 'And we'll come back in the morning to be transferred.'

'OK,' I agreed.

Back at his we got into bed, and Anthony held me all night.

'I love you, baby,' he said. 'I'll find the person who did this and I'll do the same to them.'

The next morning we went back to the hospital for 8 am. From there, I was transferred to Norwich. Without a phone I couldn't ring Mum and Dad, but I called Amie from Anthony's phone, asked her to tell them what had happened. She was on the phone five minutes later, saying they were all on their way.

'But Anthony better be gone by the time we get there,' she warned. It sounded like my parents had already put two and two together and suspected the same as the police, that Anthony was involved.

But how could he be? It wasn't possible. It was a random attack; nothing about him being involved made any sense. Still, I told him he had to leave. He knew why.

By the time they arrived, he'd gone. When they came into the room the nurse was re-dressing my wound; they saw for themselves the full extent of the stabbing, how my flesh hung limply from my face. Mum's hands flew up to her face, but even her shock did little to disguise her fury.

'What on earth were you doing with him?' Mum cried.

'He's got something to do with this,' Dad raged.

'He hasn't!' I insisted. 'He protected me!'

But they wouldn't hear it. Amie was too upset by the state of me, she couldn't stay in the room, particularly when Mum turned on her.

'Did you know she was seeing him?'

'No!' Amie lied.

The nurse got me ready for the operation while Mum and Dad were still insisting Anthony was involved. But when they took me down to theatre, just as they were about to administer the anaesthetic, the operation was cancelled because they had an emergency. I was told to go home with my parents and come back the following morning.

I went home with Mum and Dad with more butterfly stitches to hold my face together. At home with my brothers the house was chaos. Mum and Dad were still raging, and now my brothers were too, everyone insisting that Anthony was responsible for what happened. I defended him until I couldn't take any more. Everyone was shouting, and I was tired, so tired, of defending myself, defending him. And all the time Anthony was texting Amie, asking to speak to me, asking how I was. It was too much, I couldn't cope. And then Adam burst into tears.

'Look what you're doing to this family!' Mum shouted at me. 'You're tearing us apart!'

I cried so much that I felt my face wet, not with tears, but with blood where the stitches were coming undone. I ran upstairs and locked myself in the bathroom, desperate to get away from the noise, the anger, the pain – both mine and theirs.

Mum banged on the door, begging me to let her in. But I put my head in my hands and cried. 'Leave me alone!' I shouted as best I could, the words tumbling from my wound. But she wouldn't, she waited, and finally, when I did open the door, she saw just how upset I was, her voice softened.

'I'm sorry, Adele,' she said, putting her arms round me. 'What has happened to you? I just can't believe you saw him again after everything he's put us through.'

I fell into the safety of her arms. Perhaps I was crying so much because I knew she was right, I knew I was wrong. I shouldn't have seen him again, I shouldn't have let him do this to my family. But one thing I knew for sure that no one else did, he'd had nothing to do with this attack. Nothing at all.

CHAPTER 10

REVENGE

'Whatever happens, do not let her speak to him.' Mum pointed her finger as if to emphasise the point.

Amie shook her head. Mum looked at me, under the duvet; she opened her mouth as if to say something, then thought better of it. Just the look of me, my face swollen from surgery, unable to eat anything but puréed food, must have been a stark reminder that I'd been through enough, that I didn't need telling.

'I won't be long,' she said instead. 'Dad will be back from the shop with your soup soon.'

She left then, and once Amie and I heard the front door shut behind her we relaxed into the sofa as Harry watched *Cars* on the TV.

It had been a tough couple of days, a four-hour operation to repair the muscles and nerves and flesh that had been torn from my face. Dozens of stitches inside and out, and more pain than I thought I'd ever know. They'd wanted to keep me in hospital but I was desperate to get home to my parents' house, my bedroom, not least because it was Mum's 50th birthday in two days and I already felt like I'd ruined it.

Amie picked up her phone.

'He's been texting while you were in hospital,' she said. 'He wants to know how you are, what you've told the police. He wants to see you.'

'I know,' I said. I'd got my own phone back from the police when I came out of hospital. As soon as I switched it on there were dozens of messages from Anthony, saying how much he missed me, how worried he was. He sounded genuine, and there was a part of me that needed him too. After all, he was the only other person who was there that night, the only one who really knew what I'd been through. I picked up my phone, and tried to ignore Amie's face from the other end of the sofa.

'Adele,' he said, when he answered. 'How are you doing?'

'I'm OK, in pain.'

'I've got some things for you,' he said. 'Can I bring them round?'

I looked up at Amie: she was shaking her head.

'If you're quick,' I said. 'Mum has nipped to work and Dad's just gone to the shop.'

'I'll be round in five minutes,' he said.

When I saw his car pull up outside, I went out to meet him. He passed me a massive bunch of flowers through his window; roses, lilies, the lot. He'd also got me a grey teddy bear which had 'I love you' emblazoned across it. I sighed a little inside.

'Anthony –'

'I've been so worried about you, Adele … Have you spoken to the police? What have you told them? How are you feeling? At least we can be together now – everybody knows we're together, your parents, my parents, they'll all come round now they can see we're back together –'

'Anthony, we're can't, we're not back together. Too much has happened –'

'But it's OK now,' he insisted. 'We don't have to hide any more –'

'But I was never with you anyway …'

I looked up in time to see Dad arriving back from the shops. For a moment my heart pinched inside my chest, terrified what he might do, what he might say; after all, I knew all the things he'd been saying about Anthony inside our house. Would they now come spilling out onto the pavement? But Dad just gave me a look and went straight inside. I relaxed internally for a moment. It was also my cue to go back in the house, but seeing Dad reminded me just why I needed this to be the end of us for good.

'Look Anthony, I've got to go. I just need your support right now …' and I turned and went back inside the house.

Inside, Dad was furious, asking me what I was doing, why I was talking to him.

'Why the hell don't you listen to us?' he said.

I sank back on the sofa to rest, but that evening the messages from Anthony continued, the same old thing, telling me that we could be together now, that there were no obstacles between us. *No obstacles?* I was sitting on the sofa with dozens of stitches in my face, my family broken down. How were they not obstacles?

Upstairs in my bedroom, I called him that night.

'Anthony, we just can't be together, I don't want to be with you,' I said. 'I just need your support, I need you to be my friend.'

'That's it, Adele. You're either mine or you're not, you can't have it both ways!'

'Anthony, after everything I've been through, all you're bothered about is whether we're together or not. Why can't you just support me? I've been stabbed and you were there, I need your support. You're so selfish, my family is raging, and you are just on at me to get back together with you –'

The phone went dead. I tried to call back but a message came back saying calls to that number had been blocked. I tried to text … Nothing. I checked Snapchat, he'd blocked me on there. He'd done the same on WhatsApp too, every kind of social media. I stared at the phone in my hand, puzzled. How could he do this? Hadn't I been through enough? Could he not just support me through this without making it about him? Without punishing me further by deleting and blocking me from everything? It felt like such an insult.

In the days that followed I gave police a full statement about what had happened. When Amie came round I tried ringing Anthony from her phone, but when he heard my voice he just hung up. And that hurt, because he was there that night, the only one who knew what I'd been through.

'How can he be like that?' I asked Amie. She said nothing.

A few days later, though, the police called. They'd found the knife that was used in the attack and sent it off for forensic testing. It had come back with traces of DNA belonging to Leon Thompson, a local drug user.

'We still don't know the motive,' the officer said. 'But he's been bailed.'

'What?' I said. 'But it was a completely unprovoked attack. He could do that to any member of the public. He should be locked up until the court hearing.'

But the police officer said that he wasn't considered a threat. There was something else, though.

'He didn't know you, but he'd heard of Anthony,' they said.

What did that mean, though? Lots of people in our town knew Anthony's name.

When I hung up, I used Amie's phone to call Anthony again. I gave him the name the police had given me. This time he answered.

'Do you know him?' I asked.

He said he didn't. And after I hung up I was worried, he'd said that once he knew who had done it he'd find him and do the same to him. Perhaps that's why I'd told him? I didn't know. I just wanted to find out the truth.

We didn't speak again, and I didn't hear that anything had happened to Leon Thompson, so I waited for the police to finish their investigation, and for the case to go to court.

I stayed in for the next two weeks recovering, but the following weekend it was Amie's mum's birthday and she'd booked a minibus to take everyone to a Nineties night in Gorleston.

'Come with us,' Amie said. 'It'll do you good to get out.'

I knew she was right. I'd been through so much in the last few weeks that I just wanted the chance to dress up, feel attractive again, let my hair down and forget about everything that had happened.

That night I slipped on a coral dress, tied it with a brown belt, and matched it with brown heels. I wore my blonde hair clipped up at the back, and gently patted foundation over my wound, seeing how it clogged up around my dark, thick stitches, but I wasn't going to let that put me off. When I was ready, I felt better than I had in weeks.

'Are you sure you'll be OK?' Mum said.

'Of course!'

We went to Amie's mum's house first. Her sister Charlotte was going to stay home and babysit Harry, so off we all went to Gorleston. It was a great night. I danced and danced with Amie and our friend Hannah, to all the old songs, all the Nineties hits. When Cyndi Lauper's 'Girls Just Wanna Have Fun' remix came on, we threw our hands up in the hair, singing along to all the words, but then, through the crowds and the dry ice from the dance floor, I noticed a figure at the bar, watching me – Anthony.

Suddenly my stomach was churning. Why, I wasn't sure. All I knew was that I needed to get outside. I ran from the dance floor, the girls following me, and outside in the smoking area I was sick. Moments later, he walked out of the club too, standing just feet away, watching me as he pulled on a cigarette. He didn't say anything, but he didn't need to, just the fear of him kept my stomach turning over, the bile flowing.

Finally, the girls took me back inside. But I couldn't relax any more, not now I knew he was there. Wherever we were, wherever we were dancing, I needed to know where he was, if he was near me. When it was time to leave, I was relieved.

On the way home, I got a text.

Are you staying at home or
Amie's tonight? Mum xx

Hannah lived nearby so I told her if she went home I'd go with her, otherwise I'd stay with Amie. I knew it meant she'd leave the front door unlocked just in case.

But when we got back to Amie's neither me nor Hannah could be bothered to leave. Instead we climbed into Charlotte's double bed, while she slept in her sister's bed. But at 5 am I heard my phone vibrating on the floor beside me. On and on and on it went, and without even being fully conscious I woke up and put the receiver to my ear.

'*Where the fuck are you?*'

Anthony. I snapped awake.

'You weren't meant to be out. What are you out for? You've just been stabbed!'

He was screaming, over and over. '*Where the fuck are you?*'

'I … I'm not telling you,' I said, finally.

'Tell me where you are now. I'm coming to get you. If you don't tell me, I'll go to your mum's house, I'll stab them.'

And then I remembered, Mum would have left the door unlocked, thinking I'd be home. An icy cold ran through my blood.

I hung up and immediately dialled Mum's number, over and over and over. By now the rest of the house was awake.

'Mum!' I cried when she answered. 'Anthony's freaking, he's going to come to the house. Lock the door!'

I heard a sigh from the other end. 'Not this again.'

But she hung up, promising to do what I said. That was the most important thing. My heart was racing, the fog of alcohol still swilling in my system doing little to put my mind at rest. And Anthony kept ringing my phone.

'Answer it,' Amie said. 'He knows you're awake. If you don't answer he'll just go crazy.'

But when I did, it was more of the same, more threats. And something inside me snapped. Mum had locked the door, they were safe, what could he do? For the first time, I switched off my phone, I just couldn't be bothered to listen to any more of Anthony's threats. It was a breakthrough. I lay back on the bed, and slowly the rest of the house settled, and eventually I went off to sleep.

I was woken again at 7 am. Amie was standing over my bed, clutching her phone.

'Adele, you better look at this,' she said, her face stony serious.

She passed me the phone, and on it was Anthony's Facebook page. I looked up at her, confused, my head thick with a hangover, my eyes struggling to focus. Her eyes urged me to look closer at the phone, but it looked like she was struggling to say why.

I stared again, and within seconds the video came into stark and sickening focus. Me ... my naked body ... Anthony ... the two of us ... writhing, naked ... groans of pleasure ... a shaking camera image ... but there was no mistaking it. I closed my eyes to block it out, but I could still remember when it happened, Anthony bullying me into letting him film us having sex two years before. And now he'd posted it on his Facebook page for everyone to see. He'd even added a caption: *Here you are, everyone can see the slut now.*

I threw my hands up to my face, wishing the images away, the full horror of it sinking in. And it wasn't just one video, there was another of me giving him oral sex, and another.

'Your mum called, one of Bonnie's kids had seen it on Facebook, she thought you better know.'

'No!' I cried. My mum knew, even her best friend's kids had seen it. '*No!*'

And by the looks of the comments on Facebook, so had many others. There were dozens of comments underneath it already, many of them criticising Anthony, saying he had no respect for me. But none of that mattered, not when the shame of people seeing me like that, at my most vulnerable, was swilling around my stomach. I felt sick. I ran to the bathroom. There I retched, I cried, my lip was throbbing with pain, my head spinning. What had he done? How could he have done this to me?

Amie reported it on Facebook, so did Hannah and Charlotte and Lynn. I picked up my phone and called Anthony.

'Why?' I asked. 'Why? Why? *Why?*'

He didn't answer me, he just hung up.

'How could he?' I sobbed to Amie.

'He's crazy,' she replied.

But did he have no respect for me? For us? How could he let people see me like that when he didn't even want boys speaking to me? When he went crazy if I even had a boy's number in my phone? How did it make sense that he would do something like this to me? That he would expose me like this?

'What have I done to deserve it?' I asked Amie.

'What did you do to deserve any of it?' she said.

I put my hand up to my face, a face torn apart by him, first my eye, then my mouth. All because I didn't want to be with him. That was all. Nothing more than that. It was all just sinking in. Everything.

'Come on,' Amie said. 'We've got to get to the police station. We need to report this, get it taken down from Facebook.'

As we drove to the police station, a thousand thoughts were racing through my mind. I hated the fact that, even as I drove there, more people were waking up to that video, more strangers were seeing me naked, exposed. But I thought of other things too, what Anthony had said this morning when he called ranting and raving, that I wasn't *meant* to be out, that I'd just been stabbed.

I thought back to the night I was stabbed, of Anthony running after the attacker. He did, he did run after him, he'd kicked him to the ground. I saw him. But he also let him go. Anthony wouldn't have done that. He would never have let someone who stabbed him get away. Never. I knew him well enough to know that. That thought kept going around and around in my head, a thought so terrifying forming that I didn't dare say it out loud.

And in the next second I was thinking about my family waking up to that, my parents, my brothers, the humiliation they would feel. Hadn't my family been through enough? I thought too of everything I'd been through for Anthony, how I waited for him in prison, how I'd tried so hard to make it work, how I'd taken him back so many times, even after he hurt me physically and mentally. And after all that he still had no respect for me. Or could it possibly be *because* of all that, he had no respect for me?

In the next moment I was back to the night of the attack, that same nagging thought getting bigger and bigger and bigger in my mind, taking up so much space until I couldn't possibly ignore it. Anthony hadn't saved me that night I was stabbed, he'd planned it. I knew that now. Why else would he humiliate me now? Why else would he want to hurt me so badly, unless he hated the very bones of me. I sank back in the passenger seat and closed my eyes. There was no escape from my life; there was no way out, or not one that I was willing to take. Anthony would haunt me in whatever form he could. I was slowly suffocating in my own life.

Those awful videos were finally removed by Facebook after four hours, but by then they had been there long enough for everyone to see – including the police. I gave a statement, but it took police three days to arrest Anthony. Once they did, he told them that his phone had been stolen and he hadn't posted the videos on Facebook. So the only thing he was charged with was harassment. But history told me that wouldn't change anything.

News of what had happened quickly spread through social media. Even when the videos had gone, people were still updating their status on Facebook with the likes of OMG, can't believe what I woke up to this morning!

I hated the fact that everyone was talking about me, and especially because of those disgusting films. I was humiliated, burning with shame, and anger. I couldn't bear to go out that weekend, or even the one afterwards. I just wanted to hide, to run away and hide, but there was nowhere to go, so instead I found sanctuary at my parents' house, in the safety of my bedroom.

I knew of course that Anthony could still get to me there, that any day a message from him could ping into my phone, interrupting the peace I had created. And yet, they never came. Not one message or phone call, nothing pleading, nothing nasty either. For the first time I wondered whether this was really it; that he was going to leave me alone now. But instead he infiltrated my head in a different way. I let him in by constantly going over things that had happened over the last six years, asking myself what it had all meant, if he had ever loved me. Finding evidence to prove it one way or the other. But the one question that lingered longer and louder than any other was: why?

It took me six weeks to go out again, long after the stitches were removed, just a night out with my friends, and because I hadn't been drinking for so long I got absolutely plastered. Through the fug of alcohol I remember seeing a figure in the club watching me, somehow knowing it was Anthony, but we didn't speak. And still I didn't hear from him.

A week later, I went out with a friend from work for a drink. I saw him again there, again just watching me, not coming over, but it marked the end of the night for me; without my best friends around me, I didn't feel safe.

The following day, though, a message came through on my WhatsApp. There were no words, just kisses and lovehearts. I looked at the photograph; it was of an Indian guy. I had no idea who.

Who is this? I wrote.

They replied back with hearts and kisses.

I pressed them more. *Who is it?*

Nothing but hearts and kisses back.

I ignored the messages then, but I saved the message under X? Just in case …

Weeks went by and still nothing from Anthony. Only one day, towards the end of July 2014, I was flicking through my WhatsApp when I saw the message from that strange number, the one I had saved as X? I looked closer; it looked from the thumbnail like the picture had been changed. I clicked on it and enlarged it. I recognised the face instantly: Anthony.

So he had tried to contact me, but he had also gone away again, so I forgot about it, but I kept the number, just in case anything happened.

On 9 August, a few weeks later, Mum and Dad left for a holiday in Turkey, and that night I went out for a drink with my friends to a local pub where Amie was working. We had a good night, but I saw that Amie had one eye on the back of the pub.

'What is it?' I asked her.

'Anthony,' she said. 'I've seen him looking through the windows, watching you.'

When I turned around, I couldn't see him though. But I didn't feel scared, I knew he'd always be there, in the background, but could it be that we could finally exist in the same town together, that I could finally move on?

For the first time I didn't miss Anthony. So many times I'd tried to get over him before, and yet the pull of him remained. But not now, not after what he had posted on Facebook. If before I'd told myself that whatever else he'd done at least he loved me, now I knew for certain that he couldn't have done. Not if he let people see me like that. A tie had been severed between us permanently; and yet … and yet, I was still so desperate to make sense of what the last six years had meant to him. If it wasn't love, then what was it for him? Would I ever understand? Would he ever tell me? Could I rest unless he did?

The following day, I was at home, the house to myself, when a message beeped into my phone.

X.

Anthony. I'd had enough.

Adele: Please just delete and block me. After everything you still try and get to me and fuck my head up. This can't go on any longer it's doing me in

Anthony: Same, but don't think either of us can delete it hey :/

Anthony: One last cuddle and then we can delete and block each other?

Adele: Do you really think I'd come near you after what you did??? The thought of touching you makes me sick.

Anthony: Bullshit. One last cuddle and then I'll delete ya ...

Adele: Like I wanted a cuddle when I got stabbed. But no ... You're that selfish you thought I needed more shit.

But he kept asking, completely oblivious to the fact that after everything he'd done I just didn't want anything from him any more. And yet, the chance to speak to him, to ask him some of the questions that had been going round and round in my head for weeks was too tempting.

Adele: You have ruined everything and you're still trying to fuck my head up. I just want you out of my life. I trusted you most out of everyone, and yet you hurt me the most, no apology, nothing ... I can't believe what a mug I was to ever think you loved me. All those promises, yet I get black eyes.

Anthony: I don't really expect your forgiveness Adele, never will, all I really wanna do is give u one last cuddle and say bye, I think we both need to do it and walk away and realise how much we love each other it will never work ... don't care wat u say I no u love me and I no u hurt same as I do but we both no it's done ...

Adele: Don't even act like you know me. You don't know me at all.

Anthony: Tell me honestly,
do u never think bout me?

Adele: Honestly, only time
I think about you is going
through all the bad stuff
you did.

Anthony: Bullshit ... I just
wanna give you one more
cuddle.

I knew inside that I shouldn't be talking to him, but for once I
felt I had the upper hand, that I was the one with the power
this time because I knew, after what he'd done, I'd never go
back to him.

Adele: Honest question.
Did u love me?

Anthony: With all my
heart. U?

Adele: Then please leave
me alone.

And still he went on.

Anthony: Cuddle.

Adele: You're just a
heartless person who
doesn't have feelings and
doesn't care about anyone
else other than yourself and
your reputation. Look at
the state of you, you try to
be someone you're not. I
feel sorry for you. I used to
stand up and say I know the
real Anth deep down. But
truth is the real Anthony is
a messed up bully who just
hurts people to make
yourself feel good.

Anthony: LOL. Bully? Now
u just taking too far u just
taking ya anger out.

It was the first time I'd ever told him exactly what I thought
of him, the first time I'd ever felt brave enough, and it felt
good.

Adele: I can't see if you
loved me how could you do
what ya done. I go through
it in my head constantly.
You didn't love me.

Anthony: Fair enough, if that's wat ya think

Adele: Actions speak more than words. Can't even give me an explanation can ya?

Anthony: Wat for? Cuddle

The text messages went on for three days on and off.

Adele: I just want answers. Nothing else

Anthony: Then we meet nd talk

Adele: No. Wouldn't ever meet you. I wouldn't help you even if you was dying

Anthony: U can stay on ya high horse babe honestly, u bore me to death u are a mess of a girl, no tits, smashed in saggy bucket nd a massive rep for being a easy slut, u aint really going anywhere in life LOL. I ain't mr perfect but I'm pretty well off, in good shape, got my own businesses and have perfect son ... I got all the evidence I need baby to get off with the last charge ur apparent harrassment charge nd according to my lawyer ur texts will get me walk, so my job is done beautiful so whatever u say or don't say don't think it hurts cos I laugh, all I wanted was to stay outta jail, u aint worth a second of my time u was a nothing nd always will be

Adele: Like I said, I couldn't
care what happens to you.
Least of my worries! You
can comment on me all you
want but I was fine when I
was with you

Anthony: U damaged goods
babe, wen think bout it wat ya
got no tits, saggy bucket,
fucked face now nd a stupid
horse that all sluts carry
round :) dw babe every one
will make u feel special till
they smash ya in, all men do.
Like I said I've print screened
it all so u can delete me or
whatever or keep texting all
better for proving wat a lying
cunt u are

He sent me screengrabs of our conversation. So that's what it
had all been about, goading me into a conversation so he
could get off his harassment charge. But I had something
more than that, I had my dignity. He'd thrown all those
insults at me. Even after everything he'd done he still needed
to talk to me like that, to gloat about my face, something I was
more and more convinced that he was responsible for.

That last conversation we ever had pretty much summed
up Anthony Riley.

CHAPTER 11

THE ATTACK

14 August 2014 was warm and sunny. There was not a cloud in the sky. Instead, as I walked our Jack Russell, Alfie, in the alley at the back of our house, I looked up into a clear day. The deep blue was interrupted only by the thick white lines that planes carved through the sky above me, and watching them made me think of Mum and Dad on holiday in Turkey. They were two hours ahead there. Perhaps they were just getting up for breakfast in their hotel, preparing for a day sunbathing on the beach, I wondered, as Alfie sniffed around in the grass.

It seemed a shame to spend such a sunny day at work, and I envied my parents their break, but yesterday had been my day off and I'd spent it beautifying myself; I'd had my new pink acrylic nails put on and I'd sat patiently while the beautician applied eyelash extensions. I'd also burnt my backside by staying too long on the sunbed. I winced again at the pain and typed out a text to my friend, Hannah.

Don't know how I'm going
sit at my desk all day with
my burnt bum! :-) LOL

By the time I got back into the house, she'd replied. Strange that she was up so early too as I thought she'd booked today off work.

Once I'd given Alfie his biscuits, I got on with getting ready to leave for work. I felt good that day with my nails and eyelashes done, and as I pulled on my skinny blue jeans – wincing as they brushed the scorched skin on my bottom – I noticed the sunbed had done its job, topping up my summer tan. I paired my jeans with a black camisole top, and over the top of that I slipped on a blouse with three-quarter-length sleeves over the top – that way I could show off the bit of tan that was poking out on my forearms. I put my make-up on in the mirror; my blonde hair now reached past my shoulder, and I wore it down; and then, by around 8.10 am, I was ready to leave. I grabbed my black plastic Ted Baker tote on the way out, slipping my purse and make-up bag inside so that it wouldn't feel so empty.

I walked out of the house and up the road towards the bus stop, the same one where I'd waited for my friends so many times before, the same one that Mum had walked me to when her hand felt so big in mine. As I did, I dialled Hannah's number so we could chat as I walked to work. It wouldn't take more than half an hour, and it would be nice on this sunny day, but as I approached the bus stop I saw an elderly couple standing nearby in a patch of sunshine and realised that must mean a bus was due any minute.

As I walked the final few feet to the bus stop, chatting to Hannah, cars swept by on the main road, commuters busy getting to work, driving on autopilot just like they did every day. I took a seat at the bus stop, and looked up the road in the direction the bus would be coming from. As I did, I noticed a man walking towards me, and even though Hannah was chatting in my ear, he caught my attention perhaps because he looked so out of place on our street. He was wearing black trainers, a black tracksuit with some sort of red logo on it, he had his hood up, and a black scarf over his mouth and nose. It seemed so odd to me on such a sunny day – who would dress like that? He was holding something too, a bottle – perhaps a bottle of Lucozade, I guessed – I couldn't see, and he was shaking it.

He got closer, and as he did, some kind of instinct made me twist my body and legs inward towards the bus stop to allow him to pass. I glanced up at him as he passed, and as he did he looked down at me from underneath his hoody and scarf, a pair of eyes looking out at me, a pair of eyes looking *right* at me. Had I not been chatting to Hannah, I might have paid more attention to them, I might have turned and watched him walk up the road in the opposite direction, but I was just relieved when he'd gone by. I didn't know what it was about him, but it had made me feel uneasy. Seconds later I was distracted again by something Hannah said and forgot all about him.

We chatted some more as I looked up the road waiting for the bus, and then there came the moment when everything changed. What do I remember? I strong instinct to turn away, perhaps a shadow in my peripheral vision, I don't know. But as I chatted to Hannah, holding my phone in my right hand, something told me to move myself away, to look down, to pull my face into my left shoulder. Did I, in that split second, feel a shadow approach me from behind? Was that what made me look away? Or was it pure fluke? Because a second later I felt the splash of what appeared to be water thrown across my face, into my hair, and all over my right hand.

I threw the phone down mid-conversation, watching it clatter to the floor, and I jumped up from the bus shelter. The first thought that crossed my mind – in that split second – was how I was going to go to work with wet hair, but before that thought had fully formed in my mind, before it had chance to appear in my consciousness, the burning started. And then, suddenly, I felt like I was on fire. There is no other way to describe the pain, but I knew exactly what it was: acid. This was not water; this was acid that had been thrown over me. I don't remember seeing who had done it, I didn't see anyone running away, or hear any footsteps. I felt nothing but the pain.

I ran then. I ran into the road. I ran in among the traffic. I ran in circles. I screamed and screamed because I could feel myself melting; I could feel the skin peeling from my body. I could feel my long hair singeing and curling into a crisp. I could feel the acid eating away at me – eating me alive – I could feel it dissolving and melting, and taking my face, my ear, I could feel my ear disappearing from my head.

'*Help me! Help me!*' I screamed, running in the road as more cars slammed on their brakes.

I saw in those split seconds the puzzled faces of passers-by, I saw the wide eyes of the drivers who'd had to slam on their brakes as I darted into the road. I saw people slowing down as they walked past the bus stop, standing on the pavement, watching as I ran wildly one way and then the next, screaming, burning.

As I ran I could see smoke following me, I could see that I was burning in front of people's eyes, in front of my own eyes. There was no distinguishing one part of me from another, there was only white, raging pain.

'I'm burning! I'm burning!' A scream that I didn't recognise as my own escaping from me.

Suddenly, I spotted the old couple who had been waiting beside me near the bus stop. I ran over to them, stock still in their patch of sunshine. I grabbed hold of the old woman's hands and I pleaded, I begged for her – for anyone – to help me.

'Help me!' I screamed. 'Call an ambulance!'

But it was as if that second stood still for her, the horror in her eyes unable to form a single thought, or utter a single word; instead she looked down to where I was holding her hands, and she screamed as she saw that the pink liquid I was covered in was dripping from me onto her flesh, that it was melting her skin in front of her eyes.

'My God! My God! It's on me!' she cried.

And then her husband stepped forward, and she wasn't there any more. And I was running somewhere else, across the road, back the other way, zigzagging among the traffic, trying to run away from my own body, my own pain. I looked down at my eyes and saw the pink gooey liquid had scorched through my clothes, and was seeping into my skin, burning, melting, making it one indistinguishable scene of horror. My brain was trying to make sense of the images and the pain. I was dying, I had to be, this had to be what it felt like.

My entire body felt like it was on fire, and still the pain kept coming. I could feel the liquid dripping from my hair, down my back, penetrating new skin, eating away at different, new flesh. I looked down at my chest and saw that my bra had been burnt away by the acid, curled up like scorched paper; instead it hung on my chest, my skin a molten mess among it. My blouse was gone, or at least I couldn't see it because my skin – or what had once been my skin – was exposed and pink and gooey, burnt away.

I heard all around me the screech of brakes as more cars stopped in the road to look, to help. I saw people getting out of cars, their shocked faces scrambling to make sense of what they could see.

'Call an ambulance! Call an ambulance!' I cried again. By now half a dozen cars had stopped, people had got out of them, they were standing watching, horrified, and yet when I ran to them they backed away, terrified I'd touch them too, that the acid would take their skin. They were scared, I saw it in their eyes.

I ran across the road to the pub, a plume of smoke following me.

'Water! Water! Give me water!' I cried.

Then someone appeared with a huge jug, and with one giant heave they threw it over me. If it offered a split second of respite from the agony, I wouldn't know, because by now it was hard to distinguish anything from the pain. It was all-consuming. It was consuming me, literally. I was drenched, I felt the water dripping down my face, down my back, and then I felt more pain, more burning, the water mingling with the acid and burning even more of me in new places, new skin.

And the smell … the smell … It is not something that I could describe, it was awful, it was deathly.

With the water in my hair, the acid dripped further down my body. I looked down at my jeans and saw big holes scorched through them, the flesh underneath them red and angry and dissolving in front of my eyes.

A woman ran from her car then, leaving the stunned driver sitting in her seat. She ran right up to me. She was wearing a uniform from a bank, I remember her name tag said 'Mandy', she was sobbing, her hand flying up to her face.

'You're going to be all right,' she said, over and over. 'You're going to be all right.'

And I would have believed her if she wasn't crying so much, if her face had done anything to hide the horror of watching me melting alive.

And then there was someone else, a man, someone angry.

'Stop crying! You're making her worse!' he told the woman.

And behind them more people, more strangers, all of them stopped in their tracks on their way to work, and in among them me screaming in agony.

People were rushing out of their houses, stripping their jackets and cardigans off to offer them to me. Someone ran out with a blue deckchair, they sat me on it, wrapping jackets around me one after the other, but the acid continued on its evil mission, burning through them one by one, trying to get to me. As quickly as it ate its way through one jacket, they replaced it with another, and another, and another.

I knew that the acid had already claimed my ear, I could feel it was gone, and I didn't know how much of my face was left. All I knew was that I was burning alive, I was dying, I had to be.

'My phone!' I cried. 'Get me my phone! I want my brother … I want Adam …'

And then somewhere in the distance I could hear sirens and I hoped and prayed through my panic, through the raging pain, that they were coming for me, because I needed someone to save me.

'The ambulance is on its way,' someone said. And I willed it to hurry through the traffic, to get to me while there was still something left. Because as I sat there on that deckchair, watching more and more of my flesh disintegrate, my arm turning to a red, raw, gooey mess, I knew exactly who was responsible for this, even in those horrifying, painful moments. I knew who it was: it was Anthony.

CHAPTER 12

THE HOSPITAL

The paramedic sank down on the tarmac beside me.

'I'm Mickey,' he said, slowly, clearly, calmly. 'Can you tell me your name?'

'Adele. I'm burning! I'm burning!'

'Right, Adele. It looks like you've been burnt with a chemical. I need to get you into the ambulance. We need to get these clothes off you.'

His calm words were like a lifebuoy in the crashing waves of my pain, giving something to anchor myself to.

'I want my brother. You've got to ring my brother –'

'I understand, but for now we just need to get these clothes off you. You've been burnt with acid.'

In the ambulance, the needle that he sank into my arm did little to take away the pain, mostly because the shock had kicked in, and that made my heart race, made the pain burn deeper, brighter.

'Adele, can you help me get these clothes off you?'

I looked at him, the way you look at air hostesses on planes when there is turbulence. If they look calm, you worry less. But his eyes betrayed a fear.

'I want my brother,' I sobbed again.

'We need to get these clothes off.'

His voice was firm, cold, perhaps his calm exterior disguising a panic he felt too. But when I looked down at my chest I couldn't see my blouse or my bra any more. The material was burnt and disintegrated; what was left mingled with raw, scorched skin. He helped me undress, pulling off my skinny jeans that the acid had burnt holes into.

'My legs are hairy!' I squealed momentarily, bizarrely wanting to shield them from him. I had a holiday booked to South Africa for just a few weeks later and I had been planning to get them waxed, and my embarrassment at someone seeing them cut through the agony. Perhaps it was the shock that did it. But it didn't matter anyway, my skin underneath them was red and angry. I sat there naked, burning, on fire, and yet shivering, the shock making my teeth chatter.

We sped through the town, the sound of the sirens wailing in my ears as I sat naked and burning alive in the back of the ambulance. As we crossed Bascule Bridge I felt the bumps underneath the wheels of the ambulance, and as I did I heard Mickey speaking to my brother on my phone, telling him we were on our way to hospital. Adam worked not far from the bridge, so I knew he'd be moments behind the ambulance.

And then suddenly I felt too tired. My eyes wanted to close, the pain was overtaking me, I drifted … I drifted …

'Adele! Talk to me! Please, Adele, keep talking to me!'

My eyes shot open, but by now the shock had stolen the voice from me. I was tired, I just wanted to close my eyes again. But Mickey wouldn't let me. I found the sound of his voice exhausting.

'You've got to keep speaking to me,' he said.

But what was there to say? What was there but a world of pain? It was too much.

Everything that happened when we arrived at A&E feels like a blur now. Suddenly there were people all around me. I was hauled out of the ambulance on a stretcher ... rushed down a corridor ... the lights on the ceiling whizzed by ... more and more faces appearing in my eyeline ... medical terms I didn't understand ... words of reassurance ... but mostly strangers. I wanted my brother, I wanted Amie, I wanted my parents. And there was still the pain ... the pain. I was so frightened.

'I've lost my ear, haven't I?' I said, over and over. 'I've lost my ear, I know it.'

The nurses looked at me. 'No, it's still there,' they insisted. But it didn't feel like it.

If I thought the pain was over, that they would top me up with anaesthetic and let me curl up in a ball, I was wrong. Instead, I was heaved up from the stretcher and led into a shower. There I stood while gallons and gallons of cold water were rained down on me. There was momentary relief on the skin that was burning, but the rest of my body was freezing. Of course I couldn't see my face, but one glance down at my arm or my legs was enough to tell me what it might look like. The skin was burnt a brownish colour, like it had just disinte-grated in huge patches, the skin underneath was red and raw, and each minute, each second, I looked down it seemed to have spread.

And still the showering went on. Hour after hour. Every so often they pulled me out to test the pH levels in my skin, and each time it just showed up as zero – acidic – each second that went by, my flesh was being eaten away. I was sobbing and yet they pushed me back under the water – there was no choice, even though I wanted nothing more than to lie down, not face this humiliation of standing naked under this freezing water. I wanted to just lie down and go to sleep, escape the pain, escape it all.

'Where do you work?' one of the nurses tried. 'Got any nice holidays planned? How many brothers have you got?'

I just wanted to scream at them to shut up – and I did – because I didn't want to make this ridiculous small talk. I just wanted to lie down, to escape from the pain. And I wanted my brother, Adam.

'He's here,' one of the nurses said. 'You'll be able to see him soon, but we need to get this acid off you first.'

So I carried on standing there – for three hours in all – and each time I got out of the shower they checked my pH levels and then put me straight back in. It was exhausting, and pain-ful. And even when they did finally lie me down on a bed, when I thought I was just that much closer to seeing my brother, a nurse would come along with a pH stick and test me again – on my ear, my face, my arm, my leg – and it would have immediately dropped down to zero again, so they'd douse me in water, drenching the bedclothes and my NHS nightgown, and then I'd have to get up and they'd strip the bed and change me.

And all the time I just sobbed and sobbed because I was still burning, still crying in agony; and it wouldn't stop spreading across my skin, I was helpless to stop this acid eating me alive. I went through countless hospital gowns like that, I got up shivering and shaking from the cold, from the shock, I don't know how many times, when all I wanted to do was lie down. Then finally, in came Adam, and my tears came again, one after the other.

'It's going to be all right,' he said. But I could see from the shock on his own face that he didn't believe the words that left his mouth. Instead he swallowed hard and tried to keep tears from his own eyes for my sake. Scott was there too; his face told me just how bad I looked, but I didn't want to see, I didn't want to look in a mirror and know what had been taken from me.

'I know my ear has gone,' I said to them.

'It's there, it's still there,' they insisted, just like the nurses had. But I didn't believe them.

It wasn't just my brothers at the hospital. Adam told me his fiancée Sarah was there, and my cousin, Sophie, was there and Remi and Hannah, too. As I'd been on the phone to Hannah when I was attacked, she'd heard the screeching of cars, my screams, the sirens, and she'd known something was wrong. She was still in her pyjamas when she turned up at the hospital. My Uncle David and Aunty Tracy were there too as my parents were on holiday, but only two people were allowed around my bed at any time. Everyone who filtered in to see me, one after another, couldn't contain the tears that fell down their cheeks. I cried with them, the full shock of what had happened to me only just starting to sink in. But I just wanted Amie; no one could get hold of her but I knew she was the only one who would tell me the truth, the only one who would tell me just what had happened to my face.

'What are we going to tell Mum and Dad?' Adam sobbed.

'I'm all right, don't ruin their holiday —'

'Adele, we have to tell them.'

I knew he did, because I needed them, I wanted my parents, I wanted my mum, and just that thought made me start sobbing all over again.

'The police are here, they want to speak to you,' Adam said. But when he told me the detective who had turned up, I told him I didn't want her here.

'She's the detective who was assigned to my stabbing.'

But Adam said I needed to speak to them, I had no choice.

She came into my room in a brief moment where I'd been laid up on the bed after another shower.

'Anthony is behind this,' I told her, and she nodded. She said they'd be speaking to him. And meanwhile, the pain continued.

I couldn't see very much outside of the windows of the ambulance, just the odd flash of lightning, but I could hear the thunder, I could feel us swaying, I could hear the rumble in the sky above. I was being transferred from James Paget Hospital to a specialist burns unit at Broomfield Hospital two and a half hours away in Chelmsford, Essex. Amie and my Aunty Tracy were in the ambulance with me, and my brothers were meeting us there. By now, the pain had been dimmed slightly by the morphine drip that was attached to me, and it made me feel so sleepy. I just wanted to close my eyes, to rest, but I had already been told that as soon as I arrived at Broomfield I would be having my eyes flushed: some of the acid had got into my right eye and doctors needed to make sure they saved my sight. More discomfort, more pain.

When we arrived at Broomfield, I stood stock still as nurses took photographs of my burns, and I stood there, sobbing, as they snapped away as if I hadn't already been through enough.

'Is my face a mess?' I asked. 'Have I lost my ear?'

'You'll be OK,' the nurses said. This was the same generic answer I'd got from everyone.

After my eyes had been flushed through with liquid, I was taken to a room on the ward. When I walked in, my sight instantly fell on a mirror on the other side of the room.

'I don't want to look at it!' I said, throwing my burnt hand up to my face. 'Take the mirror out!'

'It's OK, it's OK,' Amie said quickly, and somehow with superhuman strength she ripped it from the wall and took it out to reception. I wasn't ready to see what had been done to me. So I sat there, looking down at my arms and the flesh that a few hours before had been pink and raw and now appeared to have deepened into dark purples.

'What's happening to my skin?' I asked one of the nurses, panicked.

'The skin that has been burnt is dying,' she said. 'Eventually it will go black and then we will cut it off and replace it with skin grafts. For now we just have to wait.'

They couldn't dress my injuries for 72 hours; instead they doused me every fifteen minutes with an alkaline spray which neutralised the acid – nothing like the crude shower they had at James Paget Hospital. But each time a nurse came to put the spray onto my ear – rubbing it very gently, ever so gently – I just knew that it wasn't a part of me any more. I don't know if it was the way it felt, or didn't feel, or the sound it made, a subtle squeak, as if you were polishing plastic, not flesh.

'It's gone, hasn't it?' I asked, tears rolling from my eyes. It felt rock hard to me, as if nothing they were doing was bringing it back to life. But the same generic answers came and no one was ready to let me face the truth.

My brothers finally got hold of my parents that evening, and they rang on my uncle's mobile phone to speak to me.

'We're on our way,' Mum said as I cried down the phone.

There were no flights until the following day.

'I'm all right,' I tried to insist, the small sob that escaped from me doing nothing to put Mum's mind at rest.

'We'll be there soon, Adele,' she said.

My uncle and aunt were meant to be going on holiday that day, but they postponed their flights and refused to go until Mum and Dad were back.

'We're not leaving you,' Uncle David insisted. And all I can remember is sobbing and sobbing, that day just passing in a blur of tears and pain.

I longed for sleep, but at half past ten more medical staff came into my room.

'We've got to shave your hair,' the nurse explained gently.

'No!' I cried, my hands flying up to hold onto my head, and instead of long tendrils feeling something other, something stubby and singed that didn't feel anything like my hair. Somehow to me, despite everything else I'd been through, that was the worst thing that anyone could have said to me at that time. My skin was burnt from my face, and yet I wanted to preserve the last bit of dignity I had and keep my hair. But what was left of the acid was clinging to it, and it was seeping into my scalp, burning deeper and deeper down towards my skull. There was nothing I could do but agree.

Sadly, I nodded my head, and the nurses helped me into a wheelchair. In the private bathroom, they held my head over the bath as they carefully shaved the right-hand side of my scalp and I watched clumps of blonde fall into the tub around me. As I watched it fall I thought of how I'd been growing it especially, how I'd loved being blonde again, and now it was all gone. And again, there was only one person to blame – Anthony.

Even after all I'd been through that day, losing my hair seemed the most shocking. It was the one thing that pushed me over the edge. The humiliation, the full extent of what he'd done to me sinking in, and yet I hadn't even been able to see my face – or what was left of it.

It took hours for me to calm down after that. The tears kept on coming, huge great racking sobs; perhaps when they'd shaved my hair off the shock had hit me tenfold. But if I thought the medical staff were going to let me sleep that night, I was wrong. Every two hours I was woken up so nurses could check my blood pressure, my pulse, my oxygen saturation levels. And each time they wheeled in the trolley and switched on the light, I looked down through sleep-deprived eyes and my arms were turning blacker and blacker by the hour. Still the tears came, the sight of it too much to bear. My aunty stayed in the room with me because I was so upset.

'Can't you cover my arm over? I don't want to see it,' I sobbed to the nurses, and eventually, seeing how distressing I found it, they reluctantly agreed.

'It's better for the air to get to it,' the nurse said as she applied the bandages. But I didn't care. I couldn't live watching my skin die in front of me.

'I just want my mum,' I sobbed, as my Aunty Tracy held me, helpless.

The moment my parents arrived at hospital and saw me for the first time will stay with me forever. Their shock, their sadness, their utter disbelief were apparent, and there was nowhere on their face they could disguise any of it.

I'd made Adam beg them not to cry – just to see their hurt was too painful for me to contemplate – but the second they laid their eyes on me, it was impossible. As soon as they walked into the room, Mum burst into tears, throwing her hands up to her face and rushing over to my bed. Dad's legs gave way, and he collapsed onto the floor. I had never seen my father sob, and it felt frightening and overwhelming. My father, my constant, was broken at the sight of me.

'I'm all right, I'm all right,' I told them, but just one look at me obviously told them that I wasn't.

I had yet to see myself in a mirror, but I knew that half of my face was gone. Was there anything left? I had no idea, and part of me was afraid to ask. I knew that the acid had got into my eyes, my nose; I knew doctors had tried everything they could to save them. I was sure my ear was gone, but I had no idea then that so had half of my scalp and my neck.

'Oh Adele,' Mum cried, and each time Dad looked up the horror in his face made both of us sob harder all over again.

The morphine had done its job, I wasn't in any pain, and yet it did little to dull the emotional torture of seeing my parents completely undone in front of me. When my brothers came into the room and saw our parents in pieces, they started crying too. I looked around the room and I didn't understand it – everyone I loved crying for me. But then they could see the full extent of my injuries, they knew exactly what had been taken from my face, and that made me join them in tears. But then I dried my eyes.

'I don't want to look at myself,' I said, wiping my tears away. 'I'll look when I'm recovered.'

My family looked to one another, and tried to hold back more tears.

I learnt something that day: if I cried, Mum and Dad cried, so in that instant, in that moment, I learnt not to. I held onto my tears, and from that day on I refused to let them fall because of what had been done to me. All I was focused on instead was my recovery, and justice.

'It's going to be OK,' I heard myself telling my parents. I felt the need to reassure them despite everything that had been done to me. And I meant it.

Adam and Sarah had been to Primark and bought me lots of nightwear, which meant I could finally shed the scratchy NHS gowns. They'd bought various pyjamas and fluffy neon bedsocks, a fluffy coral dressing gown and matching slipper boots. It was little things like this that gave me some sense of normality; that reminded me of a world that existed outside of this hospital and the pain.

When they got back, Adam had some news.

'Anthony has handed himself in,' he said.

And I felt my heart twist inside at the mention of his name, and something else, something that made me feel just a little bit safer, knowing he was in the custody of the police. All I wanted then, among the agony, the pain – both emotional and physical – was to know he was going to stay there.

It was there, laying on my hospital bed in my new fluffy socks, that the police came to see me the following morning. Detective Constable Matt Rogers wore a crisp navy suit. He was clean-cut, not a hair out of place, and yet although he was completely professional, he spoke to me like I was a human, not a victim, not with pity, but with sincerity.

But my parents gave him a hard time: they knew Anthony was responsible for this, and the stabbing, and they thought I should have been protected after that.

'You should have done your job properly before!' Mum said. 'This shouldn't have happened to Adele –'

'Mum!' I said.

'Well, it's true, Adele …'

There was a woman with Matt, another detective, DC Debbie Newell. She usually worked on murder investigations, but she was to be my police liaison officer. I instantly envied her big blonde hair and thought of my own tumbling into the bath tub, but while they were both serious, they were also kind. I knew I could trust them.

'Can we talk to Adele alone?' Matt said.

Mum and Dad left the room, and I sank back on my pillows because I knew this time I had to tell them everything. I thought of all the times I was frightened, how I protected Anthony, how I thought that if I just kept quiet he'd leave me alone. Now I knew that wasn't the case at all.

So out it came, one thing after another. I told them about the time he held me hostage and punched me in the face, about when he hit me in the hotel room, about how he smashed up my make-up, threatened to kill me; how he'd made me get the train home from the party by threatening to kill my family. I told them how he bullied me into sex; how he insisted he film me; how he made me have sex outside where strangers could spot us.

I told them how he checked my phone; how he insisted I didn't have Facebook, or speak to boys. How he made me go home early even when I was on holiday; how he got his sister to beat me up for going to Ibiza. I told them about the messages in the days before, just to get out of his harassment charge; how he was angry with me for going out after I'd got stabbed. I told them how every single time he did something like that, he'd beg me to take him back; how he'd cry, how he'd bully me into being with him, and how I had always relented.

I told them everything, and as I spoke I realised something else, something I hadn't realised before: my whole relationship had been about control and abuse. I was a victim of domestic violence, I could see that now so clearly, and yet until this moment I'd never seen it before. Why not? Because I was so young? Because I thought I was strong and it could never happen to me? But now when I told my story right from the beginning, not having to leave out bits that I knew would upset or anger my parents, it was obvious. What had I let this guy do to me? And that realisation gave me strength; it made me ready to fight.

Matt leaned in close once he'd finished making his notes. Although Anthony had handed himself in, they had no evidence to charge him with the attack, so instead he'd just been charged with breaking the harassment order and some driving offences which would keep him in prison for the next four months. Hearing that he was locked away made me feel a little safer.

'We will find the person who did this and you will have justice,' he said.

That was all I wanted to hear, and in that moment I had complete faith in Matt.

'Don't worry,' Debbie added. 'You're going to be all right, we'll get you through this.'

For the first time in years, I finally felt safe.

CHAPTER 13

THE RECOVERY

Seventy-two hours after the attack, I had my first surgery.
The doctor explained to me how all my dead skin would be
cut away and donor skin would be laid on top as a temporary
measure. That would give the surgeon an idea of how well
my body would take to this new skin and, if it worked, they
would take skin grafts from my thighs to cover my scalp, my
neck, my face, my arm and hand.

The surgery lasted five hours, and when I woke from the
general anaesthetic I was covered in bandages. From what I
could feel, my head was wrapped in one huge bandage –
almost like the headpiece from a nun's habit – leaving just my
face poking out. All the way down my arm, my skin was
striped with bandages; only the burns on my legs were left
untouched.

'They should heal on their own,' the surgeon told me, but
my skin was a mess, a mass of different shades of red and
purple where the acid had eaten chunks of my flesh.

Every two days the bandages were changed, and when they
were I could see the donor skin for myself. It hadn't been knit-
ted together with my own skin perfectly for now; instead I

was a criss-cross of different stitches and staples, my arm – the only bit of me I could see – resembling a patchwork quilt of different tones of flesh. But at least I had flesh – for that I was grateful. I noticed, though, after a few days, I had moles where I hadn't seen them before, and it was only then that I put two and two together and realised exactly what donor skin was – it was skin from dead people, and I was covered in it. It wasn't a very nice thought at first, but I learnt to be grateful because, if it wasn't for people donating their skin after death, then my recovery could have been completely different.

There was one nurse on the ward called Hilary that I got on particularly well with.

'Why don't you go downstairs?' she said. 'Have a little walk around?'

'Can I?' I asked. I'd been so bored in my hospital bed, confined to this small room, I longed for fresh air, a taste of the real world.

'Yes! Of course!' she said.

When I told Mum, she looked anxious. 'I'm not sure, Adele,' she said. I think she was worried that people would stare at me, that it would upset me.

But I didn't care what people thought. What could they see anyway? Bandages? It didn't bother me. So every friend that visited, or each family member that came to sit with me every day, would be persuaded to take me for a walk or wheel me downstairs. A simple trip of going downstairs to WH Smith to buy a scratchcard gave me a purpose each day, and that's how I got by at first, going from one day to the next, finding something positive to focus on, something other than my ravaged body.

I did see people looking, but I didn't care because, after all, we were in a hospital where most people were wandering around with some kind of injury.

One day, as I stood outside the main entrance, a hospital shuttle bus driver came over and stood beside us.

'Blimey,' he said, pulling on his cigarette. 'You've been in the wars. What happened to you?'

It was the first time that anyone had actually asked me what happened.

'I got attacked with acid,' I said. 'My ex-boyfriend planned it.'

Just like that, no emotion, no fat on it, nothing but the stripped back, raw facts.

'Oh ... I ... er ...' the bus driver stammered. He didn't know what to say. What could anybody say? And yet, when he recovered himself, he was suddenly furious on my behalf.

'Oh my God,' he stormed. 'He should be hung for what he's done. What an evil person.'

And I stood up a little taller. It made me feel stronger to hear people – strangers – say what a terrible person Anthony was, how he deserved to be locked away forever for having disfigured me, because it was true. After that I wasn't afraid of people asking, in fact I *wanted* them to, because each person who asked me what had been done to me, and each time I answered back, it sank in a little more. I became more comfortable with my story, I embraced it even. I would tell everyone just how evil Anthony was. But there was something else, this nagging feeling, a fear, the knowledge that he was out there, that he'd gone so far as to plot this awful thing that had happened to me: what else would he do? What might he do next?

I saw him in my sleep, I'd wake from nightmares seeing his face, seeing him take mine. It seemed like there was no escape from him even though I was in here, even though I was recovering, and all I could do was hope that Matt was doing his job, that he was getting him put away, somewhere he couldn't harm me any more, for a long time. But until I knew for sure, I wouldn't rest.

After I'd been going downstairs in the hospital for a few days, Hilary suggested I go out into town. 'Really?' I asked.

'Yes!' said Hilary. 'After your skin graft you're going to be laid up for weeks. Why not get out and about while you can? And the longer you stay locked away here, the more nervous you'll be about facing the world again.'

I knew she was right.

The first time I left hospital was to visit Ian and Adele, some friends of my aunt and uncle's who lived in Chelmsford and had been putting my parents up. I just went to their house for a cup of tea, but it felt nice, normal, to be out of the hospital ward.

After that, I went shopping in Chelmsford town centre. I wandered around New Look and Primark alongside other people shuffling along with their shopping bags, my fingers brushing the rails of clothes that I'd usually be dashing into the changing rooms to try on. Yes, people looked; after all, it was a bit odd to see someone wandering around a shopping centre covered in bandages; but I didn't care. I wasn't going to let Anthony steal another moment of happiness away from me. I felt even better, knowing that I'd been attacked with acid just days before, and now I was shopping. The thought of how much that would annoy Anthony made me smile to myself.

I enjoyed my time in hospital, partly because I felt safe there, I knew that while I was in there nothing else could happen to me. And I loved all the visitors I had: I was more than two hours from home, but every day somebody came to see me. Many times five of my friends all piled into a car and came to visit together; we'd spend the afternoon playing Monopoly in the family room, and ordering Chinese take-away to be delivered to the ward. Sometimes my girlfriends would just come and lay in bed with me and we'd watch a DVD together. I plastered my walls with photos of all my friends, and dozens and dozens of cards arrived.

I was happy there. I even came to terms with the fact that my hair was gone, and asked the nurses to shave off the other half of my head in preparation for my next operation – at least then it would all grow back at the same time. The only thing I asked the surgeons to do was save the eyelash extensions I'd had applied the day before the attack. It must have seemed such a little thing to them, but it meant the world to me to have that little bit of control over the way I looked, just a little something to make me feel better when I'd lost so much.

But even though I was willing to come to terms with losing my hair, I couldn't yet face looking at myself in the mirror. I still had no idea what was left of me. I knew by now that my ear was gone, and I even tried to give that a positive spin.

'Anthony knew I didn't like that ear anyway,' I said to my

friends. 'He knew I'd never wear my hair up because I thought it stuck out too much.'

Could I do this? Could I get through this with humour? Would it make me stronger?

But I wasn't ready to see the rest. I knew the medical staff were taking pictures, so I could see one day when I was ready, but not now.

'It's mostly the side of your face,' Mum said, trying to reassure me, but I was adamant that I wouldn't look in a mirror.

I only thought of the day when I would be healed enough to look, once the surgeons had done their work. That was my focus, and the police investigations. I knew the police were doing their job. They'd arrested Leon Thompson on the day of the attack and then of course Anthony had handed himself in the next day, but I knew they could only keep him in prison on the harassment and driving convictions for a matter of months.

All I cared about was letting the police do their job so they could keep him in there, and it sounded like they were: each friend who came to visit had some news of arrests being made, or the police taking statements from them – each of my friends fancied Matt, even some of their mums – Amie's phone had been taken from her as evidence because we'd been texting about Anthony in the days leading up to the attack. It was all coming together, slowly but surely.

Almost two weeks after the attack, it was the eve of my big operation when the donor skin would be removed and skin grafts would be taken from my thigh to replace the skin the acid had burnt through. One of my best friends, Rachel, flew over from Denmark to be there with me the night before. We got a KFC and I lay on my bed watching DVDs while she gave me a pedicure and painted my toes, that little bit of control taken back when I was about to lose so much to the will of the surgeons. The following day Amie turned up in the morning, as well as my parents, and at 1 pm I was taken down to theatre.

'You're going to be OK,' Mum said, as they prepared me for surgery.

'I know,' I told them.

I liked being put to sleep, it was my parents who couldn't stand the needles, who always needed to leave the room when I was having any kind of procedure, but they never fazed me, I just saw each thing as one step closer to my recovery, and normality. I wanted to be back in my normal life so much. Although as the general anaesthetic slowly seeped into my system I had no idea of the pain I would wake up in …

Five hours later the room around me slowly came into focus, and as it did, so too did the pain. I felt the weight of new thick bandages around my right thigh from my hip all the way down to my knee, and with it a new intense burning pain that felt like my leg was on fire. I had been warned by nurses that the skin graft would be more painful than the acid burns, and they weren't wrong. I cried out for morphine but even when it was administered it did little to help. My head was also throbbing: the skin that had been stripped from me like pieces of meat had now been stitched in ribbons to my scalp, my neck, my arm. I looked down at my body in the bed and although I wasn't bandaged from head to toe I felt like a mummy.

I did manage to sleep on and off that night as the anaesthetic worked its way through my system, but when I woke up in the morning my bandages and the bedsheets had turned scarlet with blood that had seeped through. If I thought that having the dressings changed would offer me any relief, though, I was wrong. I screamed in agony, and clutched the canister of gas and air that the nurses had brought to me. Where the skin was raw and bleeding, it made the bandages stick fast, and there was no other way to get them off apart from ripping them as I clutched the sheets and screamed. I couldn't walk because the pain was too bad; instead I was stuck in my hospital bed, even the faintest movement I made sending shockwaves of pain through my body.

I could have slipped into a deep depression, and there were of course days when I would curl up in a ball and feel the tears involuntarily sliding down what was left of my cheeks. But then I would think of Anthony, and I'd sit up and dry my eyes because he wasn't getting any more of my tears. He'd had enough. It was days like that too when I vowed that I would get justice, that he had to lose his freedom in exchange for the pain that I was going through and everything I was having to endure. Matt kept me updated as often as he could; Anthony's dad's house was raided and he was arrested too. I sobbed when I heard that: just the thought that his family, people I knew, had been a part of a plan to mutilate me. But he was later released without charge.

My friends visited every day, and of course Mum and Dad were there. Adam had started a fundraising appeal back in Lowestoft and people were giving so much to help with their five-hour round trips to visit me in hospital. He'd also contacted the Katie Piper Foundation on my behalf, and partly that was because his wedding was just weeks away in October. Adam and Sarah had talked about postponing it because of what had happened, especially as I was meant to be a bridesmaid, but I wouldn't hear of it. Instead I insisted it gave me a reason to get better, I would be well by then, I would walk down the aisle with my sister-in-law to be. Anthony was not going to take that experience away from me when I'd been looking forward to it for so long.

A few days later I was well enough to be wheeled downstairs to WH Smith to get my scratchcard. Amie took me, and I was looking forward to getting off the ward, even for the shortest amount of time. As I sat in the queue in the shop, though, Amie by my side, one of the cashiers came rushing in from the back. As she did, the staff room door flew open, and there behind it was a mirror – and it was directly facing me, at the perfect height for my wheelchair.

I stared at the stranger wrapped in bandages in front of me. It took a few moments for my brain to work out that it was me; it had been weeks after all since I'd seen my own reflection. But what I could see was … my face.

'Oh my God!' I said out loud, and with that Amie looked down and saw exactly what I was looking at. She turned on her heel immediately, whisking me out of the queue. But it was too late, I'd seen it by then.

'It's my face,' I said. 'I've still got a face!'

'Of course you have,' she said.

But I'd had no idea. In my mind the acid had melted away all my features, because I'd felt it splash onto my skin, my nose, my eyes, my cheeks. I thought it had eaten away at everything, not just my ear – which I could now see for the first time was definitely missing – but otherwise my face was so much better than I had imagined. The relief washed over me in waves, as I grinned and felt my face, letting my fingers stray across my features.

'It's all still there,' I said, amazed.

'We told you it was!' Amie said.

It was nowhere near as bad as I had seen in my mind's eye, and that gave me more strength, it returned a little of my shattered confidence. Anthony had come for my face, yet he hadn't got it. I was winning this battle, and I'd make sure I won the war.

I left hospital two weeks later – I'd been in there a month in total – but the police weren't happy for me to go home to my parents: they didn't think it was safe. Until they knew who my attacker was, they couldn't guarantee my safety. They wanted me out of Lowestoft. So instead I went to stay with Uncle David and Aunty Tracy; their place was to be my safe house. It was kitted out with all sorts of CCTV and alarm systems with panic buttons that were hooked straight up to the police station.

I found it difficult. Not because I didn't want to be with my aunt and uncle, it was so nice of them to offer me a refuge when I needed one most, but because I wanted to be in the familiarity of my own home, I wanted to be with my mum and dad, I wanted to cuddle up with Alfie on the sofa. The quiet cul-de-sac where my aunt and uncle lived was such a strange place to me; it wasn't the house that I'd been brought up in, nor was it close to any of my friends. My aunt and uncle tried to make it so nice for me: we'd sit around and play cards together, they couldn't have tried harder, but I missed home.

Every two days, though, I had to return to Broomfield Hospital to have my dressings changed. It was a five-hour round trip, but either Mum or Dad or one of my brothers was happy to take me. My thigh where they'd taken the skin graft, once the bandages were removed, reminded me of one of those huge pieces of doner meat that they heat in kebab shops, but the doctors assured me it would heal.

One day, me and Adam got back from the hospital. Everyone was out at my aunt and uncle's so we let ourselves in with a key, but as we did the alarm started beeping.

'What's the code?' Adam asked me.

'I thought Mum gave it to you!' I said.

Within minutes I heard the sound of sirens, then police officers coming in through the back garden, two coming in from the front. I put my head in my hands, completely embarrassed, and yet their quick response made me feel safe. I thought back to what Debbie had told me in the hospital: they were going to make sure I was all right and I felt safer despite the fact that my attacker was still out there. It was Anthony getting away with it that I was more concerned about. The police seemed to be confident, but I knew how slippery he was, how cunning. I thought about everything that he'd got away with doing to me in the past. Who was to say he wouldn't get away with this too? I knew there were enough people out there who were scared of him, who wouldn't speak out, or he could pay or intimidate into taking the rap on his behalf. Matt had told me that much of the investigation was meeting dead ends.

'Nobody's talking,' he'd warned me.

So as much as I believed in Matt, I thought it was just Anthony's luck to get away with it. All I could do was get on with my recovery while the police did their work.

It was now coming up to the end of September, just four weeks away from Adam and Sarah's wedding. But before that, it was her hen do. She'd booked a weekend away at Center Parcs.

'Are you sure you still want to come?' Mum asked me.

'Yes,' I said.

I could see she was worried, I knew she was anxious about people staring at me, all the things I wouldn't be able to do, but I'd been looking forward to it for months, plus Sarah was only going to have one hen do.

'I'm not going to miss it,' I insisted.

Mum still looked worried when I packed my bikinis a few weeks later. But by now my wounds were healing well, the bandages had been removed, and although there were the odd patches of raw skin on my legs, the doctors were pleased with how the skin grafts were taking on my head and my arm.

Center Parcs was something that I had been looking forward to, another milestone in my recovery which had been so important to cling onto. That's how I coped in those weeks, by setting myself a milestone each month to work towards, something to get better for. So when everyone got ready to go swimming, I was determined to join them. As I slipped on my bikini I could see Mum worrying.

'I could buy you a big rubber ring and you could sit on that in the water,' she said. I knew she was panicking about people staring, but I didn't care.

'I'll be fine,' I said.

She did buy me a headband to cover the fact that my ear was missing, I could understand that some children might find that a little disturbing; other than that, I made no concessions. I wasn't ashamed by the way I looked, I'd very quickly come to terms with my new skin, my new face, everyone else would need to as well.

I did hesitate a little when all the girls jumped into the hot tub, but it looked so much fun I wasn't going to miss out. The same when they all decided to go down the rapids. I wasn't going to sit in my rubber ring and miss out on the fun. When it came to dressing up for the nights out, I bought a blonde wig from a fancy-dress shop. I didn't care that the acid burns still stretched out in long purple patches across my face, I could live with that, and I knew I was getting better all the time. And anyway, while I was out with my friends and family, sinking shots and enjoying life, Anthony was back behind bars, so who was the real winner? It had to be me.

Four weeks later, I stood looking down a makeshift aisle at Elm Barn where my brother was about to marry his wife. There were tears in people's eyes as I started to walk down the aisle, no one more than Adam. None of the guests could believe my transformation after everything they'd heard I'd been through in the last couple of months, least of all me. But strangely, one thing was for sure: I'd had so much professional help to make it to this day that I knew even then that I looked better than if I hadn't been attacked. The Katie Piper Foundation had organised for a specialist make-up artist to come up from Wales to apply camouflage make-up for the day. It was better than I could ever have done it, from my eyelashes to my lips.

'Even if you cry, this won't come off,' she said. Not that I thought I would do that.

But as I started walking down the aisle, as the harpist played Pachelbel's Canon in D, the tears just fell. I knew how far I'd come, just to be here to witness Adam and Sarah's wedding.

In the weeks before, the Katie Piper Foundation had paid for me to go to London to have a real hair wig weaved into the inch-long hair that had grown back since my head was shaved after the attack. The long brown hair was beautiful, it made me feel great after so many weeks, and it fell loosely over my new scalp, disguising the skin grafts from my thigh.

I hadn't met a lot of Sarah's family, and after the ceremony they came over to tell me how strong they thought I was. Where had I got this strength from? The only thing that kept coming back to me was that moment when I'd given my statement to the police, when I listed all of Anthony's abuse and realised just how much Anthony had already stolen from me. I'd made that decision there and then not to let him steal any more of my life, and I'd meant it.

I had quickly come to terms with my new looks, so when Amie's little toddler Harry asked, 'Where's your ear, Del?' I didn't flinch.

Instead he'd pretend to take his ear off and say: 'You can have my ear.' Or he'd say, 'I'll go to the shops and buy you a new one.'

That's how I got through those weeks, with humour, being grateful for what I still did have. Yes, I'd lost half of my scalp, and my ear, and much of the skin had been burnt away from my arm, but I knew that it could have been so much worse.

In his wedding speech, Adam told everyone how proud he was of me, and there were more tears throughout the room. But I was proud of me too. I always knew I was a survivor, but I never knew just how much strength I had inside.

I was worried too after the wedding, once the final guests had left, once the music finished in the reception, once all that was left were empty glasses and the last of the wedding flowers, was I going to break down? If this had been everything I'd been working towards, was I now going to crash? Was the full shock of the attack going to hit me, and break me?

I braced myself, but nothing came. What did come, though, was some news a few weeks later from DC Matt Rogers.

'We've charged Anthony with conspiracy to apply a corrosive liquid,' Matt said after asking to see me.

This was the best news I'd had since the attack. I sank back against the sofa as Matt told me how it had come about. An anonymous tip-off had led them to someone who claimed that Anthony had offered him £2,000 to throw acid on me and he'd refused; along with my statements detailing our relationship, and his WhatsApp messages trying to get me to meet him, the police finally had enough evidence to charge him. The only thing they didn't have yet was the person who he'd paid to do it.

'But we'll get him,' Matt insisted.

And I had to believe him. I knew I'd been right to trust him.

* * *

Six weeks later I was invited to London to meet Katie Piper. She had been the victim of an acid attack in 2008. Just like me, her ex-boyfriend had plotted to have someone throw acid over her. I wanted to know how she'd coped with it all. But when I met her, I was shocked. She looked amazing and she'd come so far, but her injuries were so much worse than mine. Surgeons had been forced to remove all the skin on her face, and it had been completely rebuilt with skin grafts. She was blind in one eye and even swallowed some acid, which meant she had internal injuries too. I realised once again just how lucky I'd been.

Katie understood everything I was going through. Even when I mentioned how hard my parents were finding it to cope, she understood and offered to get her parents to speak to them. There were many similarities in our story too: she had been raped before she was attacked, just like I had been stabbed, and like me she was so scared of her attacker that she hadn't told police.

We talked about the trial, and she knew exactly what I meant when I told her I didn't want Mum and Dad there, especially when I gave evidence. 'I was the same about my parents,' she said.

But she gave me strength. 'When you face that jury just pick one person to make eye contact with. Just tell them what happened, otherwise it can be so overwhelming if you're looking at a sea of faces.'

Her most important advice, though, was simple.

'Just keep going,' she said. 'You can get through this.'

And I believed her because I could see just how far she'd come.

Adam and Sarah came with me to meet Katie and we sat in a London hotel sharing our stories. By the time I left, I felt great. Katie was such an inspiration to me, I felt stronger than ever before. But as we stepped out onto the street outside the hotel where we'd met, Adam checked his phone and stopped dead.

'Anthony has put up a £15,000 bail bond,' he said. 'He's trying to get released from prison before the trial.'

I threw my hands up to my mouth. Anthony? Free? I shook my head. How could he taint this day when I'd felt so good, so positive?

'He can't get bail, he can't!' I said.

I could cope while I knew he was locked away. Despite the fact that my attacker was still out there, I felt safe from Anthony knowing he was in prison. If he was released, would I cope so well? Would I be able to see all these positive things?

'Let me speak to Matt,' Adam said, and he dialled his number.

Matt was helpless, telling Adam it would be up to the judge to decide. But that night, back in my safe house, I couldn't sleep; instead I lay there, blinking out at the darkness, my duvet pulled up under my chin, telling myself that the panic alarms were installed, the CCTV was there. The police would be just minutes away.

For the next few days I couldn't rest. Suddenly, the thought of Anthony being free, of bumping into him in our town, just overwhelmed and coloured everything. How would I survive if he was out? What if he came back to finish what he'd started? Once I began thinking about it, my heart would race and my throat would tighten, tears springing to the back of my eyes and that helpless feeling returning.

In the weeks before I had been speaking to the Witness Protection Programme who were trying to persuade me to take up their offer of a new identity. They explained how I would have my name changed, how I would be moved, how they could explain my scars by giving me a cover story that I'd been burnt in a house fire, they even offered to place stories in newspapers on the internet to make it seem more authentic. They explained how I'd have two liaison officers, people who I would describe as my aunt and uncle if anyone asked. It was, they insisted, the only way of guaranteeing my safety, and yet there seemed so much to lose: I'd have to cut all contact with my friends; I'd never be allowed a mobile phone; my parents would never see where I lived and would only be able to see me through a contact centre.

'What kind of a life is that?' I asked.

'A safe one,' they insisted. 'We've seen your case, Adele, and we don't want to scare you but your safety is a high threat.'

But I shook my head. 'I am Adele Bellis,' I said. 'If I changed my life, that would be Anthony ruining my life. I'm not going to run away from him, I'm going to live my life, and even if something happens, at least then I knew I lived as I wanted to.'

There wasn't any getting through to me, and they knew it. They even complained that fifteen of our family and friends were planning on going to Center Parcs in the New Year. Too many people would know I was there, they insisted. It was too risky. But I refused to change everyone's plans: this was my life and I was going to live it.

Anyway, two days later Matt called Adam. The bail application had been refused. Anthony was staying in jail. Another win for me. For now, but – just like my recovery – it would be a long fight.

Christmas that year was depressing, though. I wasn't allowed back home, the place where I'd woken up for every Christmas my entire life. Instead, while Mum and Dad had breakfast with my brothers, I had to sit around while my cousins opened their presents and wait for them to visit me at my aunt and uncle's house.

Just a few days before, I'd been told by Matt that it was impossible for Leon Thompson to be my attacker as they had CCTV of him elsewhere around the time of the attack, so it was hard to celebrate knowing the assailant was still out there four months after I'd been attacked.

In the new year, after my Center Parcs holiday, I went to see a medium called Angela. I'd seen her years before when I was back in college, and she'd told me then Anthony wasn't any good for me. What would she have to say now? I knew I'd been in the papers, and she might guess who I was, but I made an extra effort that morning to smooth my wig over my ear, to make sure I covered up as much as possible.

'You haven't got an ear,' was the first thing she said when I walked in. And then she described everything that had happened to me on the day of the attack, in great and incredible detail.

'Your attacker is still out there,' she said. 'But there is a fourth man too. His name is Danny, he has a bald head and tattoos. The police have already questioned him, but they need to question him again. You need to ring them up and tell them that, they need to re-question Danny.'

I pictured myself ringing Matt and wondered if he'd ever believe me. But there was more.

'I have a Margaret here with me,' she said, closing her eyes for a moment, and holding her neck.

Anthony's mum. I felt a shiver go through me.

'She wasn't meant to die, but she felt she needed to get out of it, she had issues. But she says, "Anthony needs to stop blaming me for his actions, he blames me for what he's like but it's not me." She says you're beautiful and he's done nothing to you, she's proud of how you've overcome everything. But she's telling me he'll never show remorse and you'll never get an apology.'

That was probably what convinced me it was Anthony's mum more than anything, she knew her son so well, even from beyond the grave if you believe that kind of thing.

I did ring up Matt when I left, and he was quiet when I told him what she'd said about Danny.

'Yes, we did interview Danny Marshall,' he said. 'I'll look into it.'

That night I looked him up on Facebook, and when I came across his profile picture I couldn't believe it: bald with tattoos, just as Angela had described him.

I felt that shiver go through my body again. She'd also told me that Anthony would be found guilty. I only hoped she was right.

* * *

While I was over the worst of my operations, I still lived with the results of my injuries every day. The skin that had been grafted onto my neck was thick and tight, and when I held my head upright it felt like my skin might tear, so I learnt to compensate for that by walking around with my head cocked to one side. I had daily physiotherapy, and Mum learnt how to massage my neck with cream, which really helped, but she was always afraid of touching my windpipe. The tightness of my neck affected lots of things, like how I washed my hair in the shower. It also stopped me learning to drive for a while because I couldn't check my blindspot. It gave me aches in other areas as my body compensated.

I'd been given a pressure garment that I was meant to wear 23 hours a day to keep the scars flat and smooth, but when I got into bed with it, pulling it tight over my head and my arms, I felt like I couldn't breathe. It made me feel claustrophobic, like I was suffocating, so as much as I wanted to get better I couldn't bear to wear it at night.

In turn I found things I didn't like about the new way I looked. Sometimes I'd be obsessed with my hand: I couldn't bear the thick scars that ran in bumpy lines across it, so I'd wear my pressure glove all the time, and all that meant was that people stared and asked why I was wearing one glove, not two. Other times it was my arm I hated, or my neck, or my face, or my wrist, which ached when I moved it because the thick scars made my skin strain when I bent it. Other times I hated the colour of my scars, the way that they'd go purple in the cold, how they'd sting and they were so sensitive, not like the skin that was there before. I turned against each part of my body as I grieved for how I once looked.

That's how I ended up at the Centre Ster Clinic for Burn Rehabilitation in Lamalou-les-Bains. The Katie Piper Foundation had paid for me to attend the clinic for a month, having physio every day with the most up-to-date equipment and methods available. Some of the money to pay for my stay there had also been raised by friends, family and even strangers. Even my friend and beauty therapist Amy Harvey did a skydive with her stepdad to raise money for me and the Katie Piper Foundation. I'd heard that just a month there would change my scars forever, helping them to heal, and with the trial only a month away it seemed like the best time to go, to have a new and positive focus instead of sitting at home.

Mum and Dad flew down to the South of France with me and we stayed in the hotel for the first couple of nights. On the Monday morning, I waved goodbye to them and entered the clinic. It was a hospital especially dedicated to burns victims and amputees, and as a result there were wheelchairs everywhere. I was given my own room and I was grateful for the privacy, but I quickly came to long for some company there in France. My timetable was packed, starting the day with stretching and gym sessions and moving on to water jet treatments, massage and ultrasound. Every day from 8.30 am to 5.30 pm I'd be having some kind of treatment that promised to work its magic on my scars.

The first day I stood in my bikini for half an hour as I was pelted with waterjets. I felt exposed standing there, looking down at the full extent of my huge purple scars as the jets were focused first on my legs before working up my arm to my neck and my face. When it came to my head, I had to hold my face to once side as the lukewarm water shot out and stung my skin. It was horrific, and cold, and humiliating. And yet I was promised it was the best treatment available.

We did group speech therapy too, each of us in turn over-pronouncing letters from the alphabet or words, but of course it was all in French and while I copied everyone else I felt isolated and alone.

At lunch I shuffled into the canteen with my tray and picked at the French hospital food, rarely finding anything I could stomach. Even if I sat down next to a fellow patient, they couldn't speak English so instead I sat alone as they chatted to one another, swapping tales – I imagined – of how they'd been disfigured.

There was one French woman I met who tried to talk to me via a translation app on our phones.

Where are you from? American? She slid her phone over to me.

English. I replied and showed her my phone.

She indicted towards her back. *I was burnt when I was a toddler by a hot drink. I come here every year for one month*.

I told her what had happened to me. But no one understood, not really. How could anyone here know what I'd endured at Anthony's hands, how could they understand what I'd been through?

I told the admin people I felt too intimidated to eat in the canteen, so every day for breakfast, lunch and dinner I ate alone in my room. It was one of the most depressing times of my recovery. And yet, even after just a few days, I realised my scars really were starting to look and feel better. I could move my neck, I could turn my head, and the thick bumpy scars on my hand were starting to flatten, the colour lighten. That was what kept me going in France when I longed for a Greggs bakery and all they had were these *boulangeries*; or when I wanted to order a burger without it being served with blood swilling around the plate; or when I had no one to talk to except the translator who was meant to help me in my sessions with a psychotherapist and yet didn't seem to understand English. I kept a diary there but it was depressing enough to write, let alone read.

And yet the treatment was working, which made every dismal day worth it. I'd never felt more out of my comfort zone, and yet I cursed myself for not having paid more attention during French lessons at school. I talked to one of my physiotherapists who seemed to have some grasp of English. I told her all about what had happened to me, about the case, what the police knew. She nodded and I felt sure she understood.

Finally and thankfully, my month in France was up, and I started packing to return home a few days later, this time feeling better than ever. Not only was my skin better and my scars fading, but I felt ready to fight Anthony in court – and win. And on 11 March Matt Rogers called me.

'We've got lots of new evidence,' he said. 'I can't tell you much now, but it's very positive.'

I could only trust him that he knew what he was doing.

There were just a few days left at the French clinic, and I'd been fitted with a plastic mask that I would need to wear for 12 hours a day. It would be used to flatten the skin so that my scars didn't heal bumpy and uneven. It was transparent, and tightened to increase the pressure. The thought of being trapped inside a plastic mask 12 hours a day was just another horrific part of my recovery. I already knew that on sunny days it felt horrendous, and each time the scars appeared pink through the transparent surface and as the mask was tightened it felt like my face was inside a vice. But it was just another thing I needed to overcome.

For the remaining 12 hours of the day I needed to wear a fabric mask to bed which was slightly more comfortable than the one I already had at home. The only time my face and head could breathe was when I was washing or having physiotherapy. And it didn't end there. Because of the scars on my arms and chest, I needed to wear a body suit under my clothes which covered the top half of my torso, and both hands. I had to wear this for 22 hours a day; the only two hours I was allowed off was to shower.

As I stood in front of the mirror in my room in France and studied myself, I wanted to cry. I didn't look human any more in this plastic mask and body suit. How would I ever wear a strappy top again? How could I disguise this body suit underneath my clothes? The only thing I could do was put on a shirt and button it right up, but I felt hot and trapped underneath. I wanted to rip it off – the mask, the suit, everything. But I couldn't. I was trapped inside here for now. But it won't be forever, I told myself.

That day I packed the rest of my clothes into my suitcase to get ready for my flight home to England. As I packed, my mobile phone rang. It was Matt.

'We've just arrested your attacker, Adele. He admitted everything before we even got him into the car. He said Anthony paid him to do it. We've got him, Adele.'

THE RECOVERY

I was buzzing. They'd got him. 'They've got him!' I told
my therapist after the call, but she looked at me blankly. 'My
attacker?' I tried. And she just stared at me puzzled. What on
earth had I been telling her the last month? But it didn't
matter because I was on my way home to my friends, my scars
had improved tenfold, and my attacker had been charged.

Two weeks later they got the fourth man, Danny Marshall,
just as the medium had predicted.

And this time I cried happy tears.

CHAPTER 14

THE COURT CASE

I took a long drag on my cigarette, and as I watched the smoke curl up into the air I noticed that my hands were shaking. It had been a difficult day, the first day of a trial that was expected to last three weeks. I hadn't slept the night before; instead I'd tossed and turned, rolling over in the darkness, checking the time on my phone as the early hours slowly gave way from the black of night and dawn bled into my room through my curtains.

I had insisted that Mum and Dad couldn't come to court. This was something I wanted to do by myself. Instead, it was my police liaison Debbie who picked me up from home in the morning, and took me into town for a cup of tea while the prosecution made their opening speeches. When we'd arrived at Ipswich Crown Court, the place was surrounded by press, with photographers and cameramen vying for space awaiting reporters who would come outside and feed them details about the case. My case. My life. They were all here because of what happened to me.

Debbie had parked over in the football ground car park and called for a car with blacked-out windows to come and collect us. I was ushered into the court through the back doors because who knew might be inside? Anthony's friends, Anthony's family. I was nervous enough about the trial as it was without having to face any of them. So I was protected, kept safe by the police.

The first day I'd sat in a witness room outside Court Number 1 and watched my video evidence being played to the court. I'd recorded it months ago when my head was still bandaged, my skin still red and raw underneath. I looked down at my arm as I'd watched the screen and, while the skin was still pink, the scars had faded, physically, but not mentally. There was still a long way to go.

And so after that first day at court – when speeches had overrun so much that I wasn't called to take the stand – I was gasping for a cigarette, a hit of nicotine that would dim the adrenalin that was pumping round my body, the trepidation, the fear, the anxiety that this was it, my one real chance of getting justice. I pulled again on the cigarette, staring out at the back of the court, but suddenly the gates opened, and out drove a prison van – tall, white, with those small, blacked-out windows, and Anthony inside.

'Oh my God,' I said, panic crashing over me. He was in there. 'He'll see me! I don't want him to see me!'

This wasn't meant to happen; he was meant to leave the court after me, but the delay waiting for the car back to the football ground meant that we'd passed within feet of each other.

Debbie shot forward and shielded me with her arms, and as she did, I glanced up at the van, knowing I wouldn't see anything, but knowing it contained him, that he was sitting in there somewhere, handcuffed, away from me, and yet so easily able to get inside my head, to make *me* feel like the prisoner. Would this trial give me freedom? I could only hope so.

That night at home I wasn't allowed to see any other witnesses. All I wanted was to call Amie or Adam, but we couldn't so much as speak or pass messages to each other. So even though they were so worried about me too, we had to stay apart until we'd all given our evidence.

I couldn't eat that night and again, in bed, I lay awake, blinking into the darkness. Katie Piper had been such a friend to me these last few weeks and months, it was she who said that she didn't have her parents at the trial either. I had to give evidence without holding anything back, without worrying about protecting them from what they might feel, from our relationship. I knew the following day I would be called to the stand. Special measures had already been put in place so that a screen would shield me from everybody in the court apart from the judge and the jury. But I was still frightened – just the thought of being in the same room as him was enough to send shockwaves of fear through my stomach.

I must have drifted off that night, though I have no idea how long I slept. But then it was morning, and I dressed for court in a black, sleeveless top which I was aware showed my injuries. I ran my fingers along the pink scars on my arms, felt the bumps where skin had been grafted on. I studied my face in the mirror, my new face, the one that Anthony had given me. I'd decided not to wear a wig, I would go to court exposed so people could see my scalp that had been replaced with skin from my thigh, the fleshy hole where my ear had sat. I'd long ago decided that I wouldn't be ashamed of the way I looked, and today more than any other day seemed the best time to stick by that assertion.

Debbie picked me up once again in the blacked-out car and we made our way to court, again going in the back doors to avoid the waiting press. In the morning the court played the final part of my video evidence, and as I watched from the witness room I noticed that despite the bandages my nails were painted a deep burgundy and I had extensions on my lashes. Even then I was determined to take any opportunity to make myself feel attractive, to do what I could, and the thought of Anthony watching that, of knowing me and seeing the things that I did to improve the way I looked despite anything he'd done to me gave me a quiet satisfaction inside.

And yet at the same time I was terrified because I knew any moment now I was going to be called into that room; that I would have to sit just feet away from him and be cross-examined by defence barristers who would be determined to discredit my story. Hadn't I already been through enough? Could I do this? Was I strong enough?

Suddenly my phone rang. It was Katie Piper.

I burst into tears when I answered it. 'I don't think I can do this,' I sobbed.

'You can and you will,' she said. She was kind yet firm. 'I did it, and so will you.'

I didn't have to tell her how I was feeling and she didn't need to ask – after all, she'd been through exactly the same – but I trusted what she was saying to me.

'This is your chance to get justice,' she said. 'Just do this one last thing and then you won't ever have to do it again.'

I was still crying when I hung up, but there was something else in my stomach now, a steely determination. I would do this, I just didn't know how.

But I hadn't much more time to think: a few moments later the video evidence came to an end, and just after that there was a knock at the door.

'It's time,' Debbie said, and as I stood up and crossed the room towards the doorway to the court I was aware of nothing more than my heart pounding behind my ribcage.

Court 1 is a very modern courtroom – not like the wooden panelled ones you see on TV dramas – and inside, the air felt immediately tight with the tension. I was led by an usher to my seat behind the screen. To my left sat the judge; he was sitting behind a long bench, higher than the rest of the people in the court. He glanced at me briefly, his eyes doing their best to convey some kindness from underneath his wig.

'Would you like to take the oath, Miss Bellis?' he said.

I nodded, but as I did the tears came, falling from my eyes as the usher held the Bible and placed one shaking right hand on it. If I looked to my right I could see the screen and nothing else, but I knew behind it, just feet away, he was sitting. In front of me sat the jury, two rows of six people, all looking at me, all studying this girl they'd heard so much about, and none of them except one young guy – perhaps my age – giving me eye contact. Did they pity me? Did they believe me? Would they do the right thing for me? I had no idea. All I knew was that the rest of my life depended on their decision.

And then it started. My barrister stood up first, asking me questions that would ease me in, going through my statements, asking me to confirm things I'd said were correct, asking me to look at photographs, getting me to confirm that items in the picture were mine.

'Thank you, Miss Bellis,' he said, and then looking up at the judge. 'No further questions, your honour.'

Two of the assailants had already pleaded guilty to their charges: Jason Harrison – my attacker – and Daniel Marshall, described as Anthony's driver. So the trial was that of Leon Thompson – the man who stabbed me – who denied wounding with intent, having a knife in public, conspiracy to apply a corrosive liquid and conspiracy to cause grievous bodily harm with intent. Anthony pleaded not guilty to false imprisonment (when he held me hostage in his flat), conspiracy to apply a corrosive liquid and conspiracy to cause grievous bodily harm with intent.

And then Leon Thompson's barrister stood up. At first he wasn't too bad, but when it came to the night of the stabbing he tried saying that, if Anthony was involved, why would he have gone back to capture Thompson?

'But then why would he have let him get away?' I asked.

And when the barrister said he had no further questions, I sucked in the stiff air of the courtroom. I'd done well.

And then Anthony's barrister stood up.

'Miss Bellis, who saw the attacker first in the alley on the night of your stabbing?'

'I did.'

I told him what happened.

'But in your statement you told police that Anthony saw him first,' he said.

I closed my eyes. He was right, I did, and Anthony did see him first. Why had I said I did? It didn't make sense. Why would I say that? The room suddenly felt closer, the judge, the jury, the barristers seemed bigger, and I seemed so small. Why had I said that?

He handed me my statement. 'Please read to the jury what you said in your statement at the time,' he said.

And there it was in black and white. Anthony had seen the attacker first.

'Thanks for clearing that up,' he said, and then he turned to the jury. 'So you see, she lied. She said she saw the person first, but in her statement …'

Suddenly the room was spinning. I wasn't the liar, this had happened to me. I was the one that got stabbed. I was the one who was attacked. I got confused. Why couldn't they see? What was happening?

I burst into tears, it was all too much, I couldn't do it. I asked for a glass of water, but when I picked it up I was shaking so much it went all over me. And still he went on: the questions came, trying to catch me out all the time, and with that my answers became confused, or he didn't let me finish, and I was crying.

'You came across as so strong in your video evidence,' the barrister said. 'And yet today you are crying.'

But didn't he understand, that was completely different, it was a room in a police station, not this court, not where what happened here would change the rest of my life. It was overwhelming, and I broke down again, sobbing into my hands. The judge looked down and asked me if I needed a break. I shook my head. I must have been on the stand for an hour and a half by now, but I didn't want to stop, I just wanted to get it over with.

And then Anthony's barrister said, 'I would like a break with my client.'

Again, Anthony calling the shots, even here. I left the courtroom, but before I'd even got out of the door a huge racking sob just burst out of me, and I knew I should keep it in, that the jury shouldn't hear me break down like that, but I couldn't help it. It was hell going through this, everything I expected and much worse, much more. I looked down at my arm and noticed that all my burns had turned purple, making them look much, much worse, perhaps because I was stressed, scared, or hot, or cold, or crying, I had no idea, but all I knew was that I couldn't go through any more of that.

'I can't go back in there,' I sobbed to my friend Kayleigh, who was waiting for me in the witness room.

'You can,' she said. 'You've got to, you're doing so well.'

'You're doing brilliantly, Adele,' Debbie said.

'If Katie can do it, you can do it,' Kayleigh said.

I had no choice. I was still crying when I went back in, but when the judge signalled for Anthony's barrister to speak, he stood up and said, 'No more questions, your honour.'

And that was that. My barrister stood up and asked me to expand on a few things that Anthony's barrister wouldn't let me talk about. He corrected a couple of other things he'd got wrong too. And then I was free to leave.

'Thank you, Miss Bellis,' the judge said. And my part was over.

The following day Adam and Amie would take the stand, and I could only hope that they would tell the truth and get me justice too.

* * *

I didn't go to court for the rest of the trial; instead I waited at home, or looked after Harry while everyone else went. Other witnesses took the stand: my friend Claire's boyfriend Zac who'd seen Anthony punch me in his car, Laura from Hoseasons who'd seen the flowers that Anthony sent me and knew that he'd held me hostage in his flat. Each day they filed into court and added a little more to my story, filling in a bit more of the jigsaw, to tell the judge and jury more and more about what kind of relationship I'd been in for the last six years.

The court heard over those next few days how Anthony had threatened and bullied Jason Harrison into attacking me with acid; he'd offered to wipe drug debts for him, and said if he didn't do it he would 'cut up' Harrison's girlfriend. The police told me privately that they felt Harrison was as much of a victim of Anthony's as I was. Harrison described Anthony as a 'walking demon'. The court heard how twice Anthony had given him acid and twice he'd thrown it away. I felt sick when it was mentioned how Anthony dipped a live mouse into the acid and laughed as it burnt and died. In the end he paid Harrison just £500 to carry out the attack.

When the prosecution's case was finished, Mum cooked everyone burgers at our house to celebrate the worst being over. After that, my parents went to court every single day. Each evening I'd watch on the news or read the newspapers to find out what had happened that day in court. It seemed surreal to me to be seeing pictures of me and Anthony in the papers or on television, of my life being splashed around the media. You see it every day happening to other people, but you never think it will happen to you. I thought back to the early days of our relationship; how I never ever would have imagined it would come to this, the two of us standing across from each other in a courtroom. But it had, and I just had to get through it.

Each day, as I sat at home, people took it in turns to ring and tell me who was in the public gallery, what was being said, and it all seemed positive. Matt seemed happy with the way things were going.

As the trial started to come to an end, it was Anthony's turn to take the stand, and when Amie rang from court to tell me that he would be giving evidence that day I felt my heart tighten in my chest. What on earth was he going to say? What would his defence be? I wondered if he'd make me out to be a liar, or obsessed with him, or some kind of psycho. But in fact he didn't talk about our relationship in court, just his drug dealing, what he had, where and who worked for him, but that wasn't anything I had been aware of. Perhaps he was just using it as a ploy to distract from the real case. The only thing he admitted to on the stand was giving me a black eye, but he said he shut the door on my face.

'There was one other thing,' Amie said. 'He said he loved you, that he still loved you, that he'd always loved you.'

Just hearing that did make my heart twist deep inside, not for the same reasons as it used to, just because I couldn't work out how it could have ever come to this. I couldn't understand why someone could claim to love you and then maim you, so nobody else could. This isn't love. I knew that, I had the scars to prove it. But did he really still think it was?

Then the jury went out to consider their verdict.

* * *

I was on my own at Amie's house looking after Harry when the jury went out. Aunty Tracy was planning on coming over at midday to keep me company because we didn't expect to hear a verdict before then. But I was just getting Harry out of the bath at 11 when Amie called.

'We're going back in,' she said. 'The jury has reached its verdict.'

She put the phone down, and left me in a daze. I called my friend Paige.

'They've gone back in,' I said. 'Oh my God, this is it.'

She was trying to get ready to come over to see me, but as she stayed on the phone the text message from Amie beeping into my mobile.

Guilty.

'It's guilty!' I told Paige, and she squealed down the other end of the phone. But then I stopped.

'Wait – there are so many different charges, maybe it doesn't mean all of them, maybe she meant to type not guilty –'

'Relax Adele,' Paige said. 'She wouldn't have said guilty if it was not guilty.'

And just as she said that, another message came through.

Found guilty for four.

I squealed again, and Harry laughed, and then Amie was calling me so I hung up on Paige.

'It was guilty for everything,' she said. 'You did it, Adele!'

She hung up and then I picked up Harry and threw him into the air, while he giggled and giggled.

'He's guilty, Harry!' I said, crying. 'We did it!'

'Why are you crying, Del?'

'They are happy tears,' I told him.

At last.

I covered him in kisses and wrapped him in a tight hug while my eyes filled with tears, and he had no idea what was going on but he wrapped his arms around me and I could hear him giggling in my ear. I was alone then, the most important moment of my life, alone with a toddler, and I didn't know what to do with myself. Everyone I loved was there, at court, I just had to wait, and so I paced the room and played with Harry, but then it just kept hitting me over and over and over: guilty.

Mum and Dad rang a few moments later. They were both in tears, and Mum was crying so much I couldn't understand a word she was saying. Then Adam called, and Scott, and Kayleigh. And Aunty Tracy arrived and we opened a bottle of wine even though it was only 11.30 in the morning, and it went straight to my head because I hadn't been able to eat a thing. But none of the others came home because they were waiting for the press conference, and speaking to reporters, and all I wanted was to have them home with me, celebrating.

So many people turned up at Amie's that day, but it was six o'clock before my parents arrived. The minute me and Mum laid eyes on each other we just wrapped one another up in a hug. After everything we'd been through, there weren't many words left.

And then there was the moment when Matt called – my hero.

'I can't express what you've done and how much it means to me,' I told him, the tears falling down my cheeks.

'I finally got you justice,' he said.

I thought back to that first day when I met him in hospital, how I had faith in him from the beginning.

'But I want to meet your next boyfriend before you get involved with him, OK?' he laughed. That was fine by me.

We all watched the news together that night, laughing at Mum and Dad on the telly and the way Matt's head was wobbling when he was talking to the reporters. Then we went out to the local pub and Remi's dad, the manager there, gave us two bottles of champagne. But among the happiness and the congratulations, between the news reports, and all the messages I was receiving or tagged in on Facebook, I kept returning to one thought: I had loved that man once, and look how it had all turned out. So yes, I had got justice, but it was all so sad.

Anthony and the three others were sentenced in October 2015. I was in two minds whether to go to court that day. Katie Piper told me that she hadn't gone.

'I felt I'd spent enough time on my attacker,' she said.

But for me it felt more important, it felt like closure.

On the day of the sentencing, me, Mum and Dad sat together in the witness room next to the court and watched everything by video. Anthony wasn't in court that day because police had a tip-off that there might be trouble, so he was appearing via video link. I watched the screen as his image appeared, and for the first time it felt like I was looking at someone who was a stranger. He was relaxed, or deliberately trying to look relaxed, he took his jacket off, put it back on, he looked straight at the camera, he looked up and around the room, but the whole time he had this smirk. This bravado. This hard man image. But that's all it was, just an image. I knew that now.

He was sitting back on his chair, slouching, as the judge handed him his life sentence, jailing him for a minimum of 13 years, and he just laughed. It was too much to watch. I ran from the room in tears. After everything he'd put me through, he was still so arrogant.

Leon Thompson was given 15 years, and Daniel Marshall, seven years for his part. Jason Harrison was jailed for four years and four months, the judge accepting his defence that Anthony had threatened him into carrying out the attack.

I knew that Jason Harrison's testimony had helped to get Anthony, but four years four months seemed like nothing, not compared to the life sentence I would have to serve.

Outside court I gave a statement to the press. My hands were shaking as I read it. All I could hear was the sound of cameras clicking around me, and, of course, my heart racing inside.

'I believe that anyone who plans to use acid to attack some-one should automatically get a life sentence because for us, as survivors, it is something we have to live with for the rest of our lives. I also feel a life sentence would help act as a deter-rent to other potential attackers. Acid seems to have become another weapon for sick, unstable individuals. It needs proper restrictions placed on it at the point of sale, like any other potential weapon. At the moment it's too easy for anyone to buy acid on the high street.

'The acid attack on me was the end result of being trapped in an increasingly controlling and abusive relationship with Riley for a total of seven years. When I met Riley I was only 16 and had no idea how a relationship was supposed to be. For this reason I intend to campaign to have schools teach children about good and bad relationships. I am determined that something positive comes out of what has happened to me. I want anyone in controlling and abusive relationships to look at me today and realise what can happen. My message to them is: "Get out now, before it is too late."'

That night, me, my family and friends went out for cocktails at a local hotel, but it was hard for me to get that image of Anthony, slouching and smirking as he was handed down his sentence, out of my head. Yet I had to remind myself, he had gone back to his cell a convicted man starting a 13-year sentence while I was drinking woowoo cocktails and celebrating with my friends. Whatever obstacles he put in my way, I had finally overcome them. He came for my face and he didn't get it. He pleaded not guilty and went to trial and was found guilty. I had won.

But mostly, he chose to ruin my face rather than watch his son grow up. That, to me, was so low. And there I was celebrating with my friends. If Anthony had taught me anything, it was not to waste a minute.

So I got myself another cocktail.

CHAPTER 15

A REAL FUTURE

The face that I looked at in the mirror wasn't the one I had known for the last 23 years, but it was one that I had come to love. I smoothed down what remained of my brown hair, leaving my bare scalp exposed, the skin underneath it smooth, yet hairless, and then I slicked on my red lipstick, rubbing my lips together and blotting them with a tissue. I stared again at the face reflected in the mirror, and smiled. I looked good.

'Are you nearly ready, Adele?' Mum shouted up from downstairs. 'We've got to go.'

I smoothed down the front of my sleeveless tan, black and white panelled dress and headed down the stairs. There my parents were waiting with Adam, all of them dressed up for the night. It was only a few weeks ago that I'd heard I'd been shortlisted for the local newspaper's Outstanding Bravery Award. Adam had nominated me, explaining everything that I'd been through in his entry, and tonight I'd find out if I had won. In my category were plenty of other people who had all overcome the odds, mostly car-crash victims but all worthy winners, so I had no idea if they'd pick me.

The awards were held at a local hotel; there were drinks on arrival and a buffet meal, and then the awards got underway. It was strange when they got to me, seeing my photograph up on the screen, hearing my story told by a stranger. And yet, it sounded just the way I would have wanted it to if I closed my eyes and thought back to those first few days at the start of my recovery in hospital. I had been determined to stay positive even then, focusing on what I could do, rather than what I couldn't; what did remain of my face and body, rather than what didn't. I felt myself bristle with pride in myself – I had come a long way. And then it was time to announce the winner.

'Adele Bellis,' the compère said.

I went up to the stage to a huge round of applause from all the people sitting around, and collected my award. Thankfully, I didn't need to make a speech, but if I had it would have been to thank the people of Lowestoft who were behind me right from the beginning. It meant so much to me to receive this award in my own town.

I returned to my seat to more applause, and sipped at my glass of wine. Then I could relax and listen to the rest of the ceremony, and it amazed me what I heard. So many inspirational people who walk around our town every day among the rest of our citizens; it was amazing to think what the human spirit can endure when it is called upon.

And then, the final award of the night; the Overall Star of Lowestoft and Waveney.

'This is a young woman who has shown extraordinary strength in the face of adversity, who has remained positive and is determined to use her experience to help others. Ladies and gentleman, Miss Adele Bellis.'

Before I'd even had time to take it in, everybody in the room was up on their feet whooping and cheering, applause ringing in my ears. Mum, Dad and Adam were standing there, huge smiles plastered across each of their faces, smiles which after the attack I feared I would never see again. But we'd done it, not just me, but them.

I made my way through the crowds and applause to collect my second award, and the tears came when I looked back and saw just how far I had come – mentally and physically. I had really done it. I hadn't let Anthony beat me. More than that, I had beaten him.

That night I celebrated with my family and other inspirational people from our town. I was proud to stand there with my scars on show in my sleeveless dress, I wasn't ashamed of the fact that I didn't have hair. I liked my new look, I owned it, it didn't own me. I hadn't worn my wig since the day of the sentencing, then I'd stood outside court and made that speech about educating young people about the dangers of abusive relationships, and I meant it. I was insistent that my scars would stand as a reminder to them – or anyone in an abusive relationship – of what could happen to them if they didn't get out.

My scars weren't just going to be pink bumps that gave my skin a new landscape. They would stand as a stark reminder, a warning sign, a chance to save someone else from going through something like I had. I had decided, if I could wear my scars with pride and it stopped one woman going through what I had, then it would be worth it. I didn't feel humiliated by them, I'd learnt to love them. In fact, I couldn't imagine a time when I didn't have them.

I knew there would be no message more powerful to school children than me standing in front of them and telling my story. For them to see what can happen in the worst kind of relationship; for them to know the signs so that they could protect themselves. There is a reason that the first eight chapters of this book are labelled how they are: among them are the eight warning signs of a potentially abusive relationship: intensity, control, jealousy, isolation, criticism, blame, sabotage and anger. Each of us has some experience of them in some way or other.

So I'd decided to take my experience and help other people, and that sense had grown and grown inside me since that day lying in my hospital bed in fluffy neon socks giving my statement to Matt Rogers, detailing over and over everything that Anthony had done to me since I'd met him when I was just 16 years old. My first boyfriend, my first relationship. How was I – particularly at that age – to understand how much I was being controlled? But I knew even then that one day, once I was recovered, it would be my responsibility to share my story with others.

In October 2015 I received the following letter from Peterborough Prison:

Dear Miss Bellis,

I know I'm probably the last person you want to hear from right now and I know a letter doesn't make everything ok. I've tried writing this letter countless times to try and apologise and explain my reasons for my actions. I am so sorry for what I have done to you. I never wanted to hurt you. I can only imagine how horrible this has been for you and the impact this has had on you and your family's lives. I'm so sorry for the mental and physical trauma this has caused you. There hasn't been a day since where I haven't thought about you and what my actions have caused. I feel so guilty for what I have done. No one deserves what I did to you and I truly am sorry. I never wanted to hurt you but I felt like I didn't have a choice. I was threatened to do what I did to you. I owed Anthony a lot of money and he threatened that if I didn't do it he would get my family. One of his friends knew my brother because they went to school with each other so he knew where they all lived. I'm so sorry.

There was several occasions that I was sent to attack you but I couldn't bring myself to do it. I just made excuses saying I didn't see you or you wasn't there. I even tipped the acid away and tried telling him I'd dropped it hoping that he would just give up but he didn't. It just made him angrier every time. The evening I saw you outside your house I just wanted to tell you everything and go to the police, but all I had going through my head was my family's safety. I honestly felt like I had no choice. I'm really sorry.

The night before it happened I'd gone to tell him I didn't see you again. He started telling me it was my last chance and if I made any more excuses then he would cut my girl-friend up and throw acid at me then send me back out to do it to you. I really felt like I had no way out. I wish I could change things, I really do. I was beaten and had a knife put in my mouth to show me they wasn't messing around. I'm sorry I didn't have the strength to stand up to him because then maybe things would have been different.

You may find this hard to believe but I am a quiet, soft, gentle and caring person. I've never hurt anyone up until now. All I have ever done is look after and care for people. I'll never forgive myself for what I have done to you. I'm so sorry for ruining your life. I've had nightmares and been waking up in cold sweats since it happened, so I can't begin to imagine how this has affected you. I feel so guilty for it. I didn't even know your name, why he wanted it done or anything. He just showed me a picture.

I know that nothing I say or do can ever take back or make up for what I have done.

I am co-operating with the police and trying to ensure that Anthony can never hurt you or anyone else again or even put anyone else up to it. I'm really sorry for all the pain and suffering you have been through and still going through now. I was relieved when the police arrested me. I should be punished for what I have done to you.

I'll understand if you don't want to, but it may help you if we meet up in a controlled environment, so I can answer any questions you may have and it may help you come to terms with what's happened and what my actions have done. I truly am sorry and I wish you well in your recovery. I hope you're going to be ok.

Yours sincerely, Jason Harrison.

The letter that Jason Harrison wrote was handed to me by Matt after the sentencing, and to be honest I felt conflicted by its contents. I knew I would never forgive him for what he had done, and some part of me felt that he was writing it more for his own reasons rather than mine. He wanted redemption, and I was afraid that I couldn't give him that, and to be honest I didn't owe it to him either.

But there was another part of me that could see, embedded between the pitiful words of each line, a man who had been as much of a victim as me; a man who had been threatened and manipulated by evil. And in a strange way, it made me feel better to think that he wasn't a nasty person, he was just scared into attacking me, like I was scared into staying with Anthony. I would like to think that one day I could meet him as he suggests in his letter, but for now that is a long way off.

As for Anthony, I would never give him the satisfaction of coming face to face with me. During the process of writing this book I sat among the letters from the beginning of our relationship, some of them wonderful and spilling over with love, some of them hard and filled with hate. It wasn't easy reading them, going back to a time when I loved that man, reading how he loved me 'millions and millions', and each time I did, I'd glance up at the mirror, at my scars, and remind myself of what he had done to me. How had something so beautiful turned so black?

But it happens, too often. One in three women will experience violence at the hands of a male partner. Two women are killed every week in England and Wales by a current or former partner. On average, a woman is assaulted 35 times before her first call to police. That is 35 times too many.

The hardest thing about writing this book was of course seeing how many opportunities I had to leave Anthony, and yet I let each one pass me by until it was too late. I felt stupid many times, I hated myself for doing it, sometimes I found myself screaming at the words on the page, and yet it's so easy to see clearly now, to take the blinkers off and see him for what he is – a violent bully.

Except even now it's not too late, because I have survived him. He hasn't won.

I know now that I was naïve to think I could save him from himself, and I want every other woman to understand that of a man who is manipulating or abusing or disrespecting them today. I want them to know it doesn't get better, it only gets worse. That they too could end up looking like me. I have made the best of things, but it didn't have to happen to me, and it doesn't have to happen to them either. They need to take the advice that I discarded, and leave while they have a chance. And I vow to dedicate every day for the rest of my life to ensuring that other women hear my story, and take my advice.

But there is one other thing that I know: the cold, hard fact that Anthony might not have finished with me yet. He came for my face and he didn't get it. Might he keep going? Might he never rest until he kills me? I don't know. I hope not, but it is a possibility. I am 24 now and I know that one day he might just take my life. Three times I have been offered a new identity by the Witness Protection Programme, and each time I have refused. Why? Because he has not and he will not beat me. I will continue to stay the same person. I will live a life authentic to me, I will not change my name or move towns or leave the friends and family I love – all the things that make me me.

Anthony stole my skin, but he will not take my identity. He can do his worst to me, and I will always fight, and always know that I lived the life I wanted while I could.

What I have now, today, is the chance of a real future, the chance to be free and to be loved properly. And while I have it, I will embrace those hopes and dreams every day. I will discover what love looks like, but I know one thing for sure:

That wasn't love.

ACKNOWLEDGEMENTS

First I would like to thank my mum and dad – not only have you both been my rock during this entire horrible journey, but you have stayed strong throughout, even putting your own lives on hold. By being positive, you managed to get our whole family through the rough journey of my recovery and finding justice. I love you so much; you're both honourable parents and one of a kind.

My two older brothers Adam and Scott – I thank you both for your dedication in aiding not only me but our mum and dad throughout this life-changing experience. You're both amazing and, as much as a little sister hates to admit it, I do love you dearly and I'm lucky to have you both. Thank you to Adam's wife Sarah – the way you have supported our family and Adam has been amazing; you're a lovely person and I look up to you. Remi, I thank you as well – not only have you been a special friend at this difficult time but you have also been a devoted girlfriend to Scott, and I'm grateful for everything you have done for me and him.

To my best friend, sister and rock Amie – I don't think I could have overcome each hurdle if it hadn't been for you being there. Thanks for keeping me sane! And then there's your son Harry, the little innocent four-year-old who makes me laugh and who I adore so much. He's kept me going …

Alfie Bellis – our family Jack Russell – how could I forget him? He can't speak but he was always there for me when I needed a cuddle and someone to cry to; pure comfort and love from him, my baby!

Without family the simple things in life can be hard, so I would like to say thank you to the entire family – all the Bellis/Waters uncles, aunties, cousins and grandad. You have helped us all and I appreciate it so much for everything you have endured. A special mention to Uncle David, Aunty Tracy, Sophie and Shannon. Thanks for letting me into your home and treating me like your own.

To some of my closest friends – Paige Manthorpe, Laura Woodrow and Rachel Kernick. At these difficult times you have never shied away and have always just judged me as the same person as I was. It's important having such close friends to trust, and I'm thankful for that. I'd also like to thank Hayley Keller. I met you when working on the cruise ships, and it's proved that the distance between us in miles means nothing – whenever I need support you're there on the phone. And to all of my other friends, old and new – thank you!

Thank you also to Ian, Adele and Jess for making your home a sanctuary – I can't thank you enough for your support to my entire family, for welcoming strangers into your home during my entire stay in hospital. To a special family – Wendy, Barry and Justin Hunt. I am truly blessed to have met such kind, caring and generous people. The love and support you have not only offered me but also my family are incredible.

ACKNOWLEDGEMENTS

I wish everyone could be as special as all you in life. Amy Harvey, who went from being a complete stranger to someone who is now a close friend – thanks for everything that you've done for me. I'd also like to mention Mandy White – unfortunately Mandy witnessed the entire attack and I'm truly grateful for the reassurance and help she has provided me.

Thank you to all my medical team – the ambulance crew and A&E nurses at James Paget Hospital, my surgeon and the nurses at Broomfield Hospital, Hillary, Faye and ward manager Kate, Doctor Frasson and his team at the Centre Ster in the South of France, and the many others who made my stay in hospital as pleasant as it could be. Thank you to my physio Sarah for all the chats and laughs. To the Operation Oxborough team from Suffolk Constabulary – DI Darrell Skuse, DC Matt Rogers, DC Mei-Lin Chan, DC Paul Miller, DC Steve Bracey and liaison officer Debbie Newell for your dedication and commitment to my investigation. Thank you for giving me my life back and finally making me feel free. To the CPS and my barrister Andrew Jackson and solicitor Nikki Miller – thank you for getting me justice. Thank you to Katie Piper for the advice, the friendship and the inspiration, and to the wonderful charity the Katie Piper Foundation. I really wouldn't know where I'd have been without you, from sorting out my wigs and treatments to meeting all my fellow burns survivors and new friends, and realising that I'm not alone.

Thank you to my editor Kate Latham and all the team at HarperCollins, my agent Jonathan Hartley for making this book happen and Robyn Drury at Diane Banks Associates.

And finally, thank you to the people of Lowestoft for your generosity and ongoing support, and to the general public from all around the world for your messages, for stopping me in the street, and for offering me so much love and support.